Gatwick Airport

Geoff Jones

Ian Allan PUBLISHING

Contents

First published 2000

ISBN 0 7110 2752 8

© Ian Allan Publishing Ltd 2000

Published by Ian Allan Publishing

an imprint of Ian Allan Publishing Ltd, Terminal House, Shepperton, Surrey TW17 8AS.
Printed by Ian Allan Printing Ltd, Riverdene Business Park, Hersham, Surrey KT12 4RG.

Code: 0006/C2

Front cover: Aircraft tails at Gatwick's South Terminal in July 1999. The control tower, one of Gatwick's most prominent buildings, can be seen in the background. Geoffrey P. Jones

Back cover: A busy South Terminal in July 1999 as meeters and greeters await arrivals. Geoffrey P. Jones

Below: The view in July 1999 from Skyview of the South Terminal's Satellite with its 'Peoplemover' Rapid Transit System linking it to the main South Terminal. The striped structures are blast walls to protect ground handling vehicles from aircraft jet blast as they arrive and depart the apron. Geoffrey P. Jones

Introduction

London's Gatwick Airport is now the busiest single-runway airport in the world. Handling over 30 million passengers per annum, with over 100 airlines serving more than 280 destinations worldwide and representing 255,000 aircraft movements, Gatwick celebrates its 70th anniversary in 2000. It has developed from a small, grass aerodrome that began life in 1930 as the home of the Surrey Aero Club.

Gatwick's transition to its present-day form started in 1952 following government approval for development of a second main airport for London as an alternative to Heathrow. In an almost unprecedented move, Gatwick was closed to all air traffic in 1956 for a huge civil engineering construction scheme which was completed in 1958.

One of Gatwick's plus points is its location alongside the London to Brighton railway line and, although 28 miles (45km) south of central London, rail and motorway links make it extremely accessible for passengers. Enlargement of the South Terminal built over the railway line, the addition of the South Terminal Satellite and then the North Terminal between 1983 and 1988, have helped the airport gain its current world-ranking status.

Gatwick was originally renowned as an airport handling charter flights and only a few scheduled operations, but now the pendulum has swung the other way considerably. Two major operational landmarks have probably contributed to the airport's present-day success. First was the establishment of Freddie Laker's 'SkyTrain' low-cost services from Gatwick to the USA in 1977, and the repercussions on British Airways' and Pan Am's near monopoly on the North Atlantic route. Then, in the Gulf War era, came the failures of Air Europe in 1991 and in 1992, British independent airline Dan-Air, which became a wholly owned subsidiary of British Airways (BA). This was the turning point in BA's growing domination

Above: *With a Pan Am TriStar on finals to Runway 26, this roadsign welcomed drivers to the South Terminal in the 1980s. The road link from the M23 motorway (and in turn the M25), together with the rail links, make Gatwick one of the world's most accessible international airports.* Geoffrey P. Jones Collection

of operations at Gatwick. By 1999, BA, its subsidiaries and franchise partners, had a huge presence. They operate 47% of the take off and landing slots, and serve 127 destinations in 66 countries including a growing number of long-haul destinations, currently standing at 47.

Charter airlines and operations still form a major part of Gatwick's traffic, however. As well as BA's huge presence, the airport is also the home of Virgin Atlantic Airways and is the UK terminus for most of the larger US airlines: American, Delta, Northwest, Continental and US Airways.

There are numerous other epithets that Gatwick can lay claim to. It serves more US destinations than any other European airport, including Heathrow, while the three most popular destinations are Orlando, Malaga and Palma de Majorca. It is one of the fastest growing international airports in the world at an annual rate of over 9% and is expected to handle around 40 million passengers a year by 2008.

For the air traveller, Gatwick is one of the most pleasant and user-friendly international airports of its magnitude. From the enthusiast's point of view, its rooftop Skyview terrace is totally refreshing, one of the few such viewing facilities remaining at any of the world's major international airports. Beneath the surface of the hustle and bustle there is still a family spirit among the employees of the airlines, handling companies and maintenance organisations at the airport,

Above: *A fairly quiet ramp area and North Terminal in May 1992. In the middle foreground with outer wings missing, the all-white ex-Dan-Air DH106 Comet 4 G-APMB now owned by Gatwick Handling for training staff in ground handling of aircraft.* Geoffrey P. Jones

many of whom have been there all their working lives and have moved through a number of employers in that time.

This book provides a detailed yet concise background to how London Gatwick Airport has obtained its pre-eminent position today. It also includes a detailed resumé of current operations both seen and unseen, a wealth of useful data and airport information, and finally, details of the aircraft and airlines currently operating from the world's 6th busiest international airport.

Acknowledgements

The author would like to thank the following organisations and people for their help in the writing and compilation of this book: Andrea Stumpf at Jeppesen GmbH, Ken Ellis, Nigel Hitchman, Mike Kemp, Laura de Vere (Communications Manager Gatwick/UK Regions) at British Airways, Diane Jones at Gatwick Guest House Association, Debra Seymour at NATS, Brian Southgate at FLS Aerospace, Anna Burdsall at Virgin Atlantic Airways, Shaun Monnery at JMC, Keith Burton, Claire Headicar at BAA, Andy Kynock at US Airways, Delta Air Lines, and many others.

Above: *A variety of scheduled and charter traffic at Gatwick's South Terminal in April 1999. Note the dominant SMVCR — stalk-mounted visual control room — in the background with the FLS Aerospace hangar to the right. This huge facility is currently sub-leased to BA for Boeing 777 maintenance.* Geoffrey P. Jones

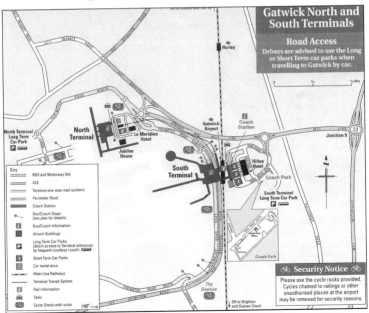

Above: *General plan showing South and North Terminals with road and rail access.* BAA

Facts and Figures

IATA three-letter code: LGW

ICAO four-letter code: EGKK

Location: N51 08.9 W000 11.3 (2.7 nautical miles north of Crawley)

Elevation: 196ft (60m)

Area: 679 hectares/1,678 acres

VHF frequencies: Gatwick Director — 126.82, 118.95*, 135.57*, 129.02* (*when directed by ATC)

Gatwick Tower — 124.22, 134.22*

Gatwick Ground — 121.80

Gatwick Delivery — 121.95** (**initial call for departing aircraft 30min prior to start up)

Gatwick ATIS — 121.02 (automated weather + other operational data)

Runways: 08R/26L — 3,159 x 46m (10,364 x 151ft) — asphalt/concrete

(ILS for 08R — 110.90 IGG 082) (ILS for 26L — 110.9 IWW 262)

Note: DME/ILS frequencies paired — DME reads zero at runway threshold 08L/26R — 2,565 x 46m (8,415 x 151ft) — asphalt/concrete

Terminals: 105 aircraft stands, 57 of which are served directly with boarding bridges at the two terminals. Other stands are served by bus rides from the terminals.

South Terminal — opened in 1958 but with progressive expansion since including much enlarged terminal building and three boarding 'finger'-type piers. One of these (the northern) was developed into the circular Satellite opened in 1983.

North Terminal — initially opened in 1988 and extended in 1991 with the addition of a second pier. In 1994, a new international departure concourse was

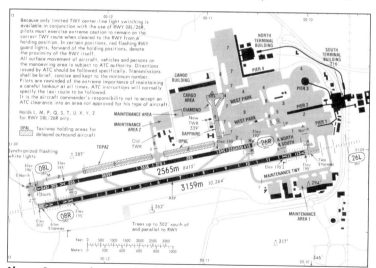

Above: Runway and taxiway plan, Gatwick chart.
Copyright 2000 JEPPESEN GmbH. Not for navigational purposes — information only.

opened which is largely monopolised by British Airways.

Ownership: Operated by Gatwick Airport Ltd, a subsidiary of British Airports Authority plc (BAA), a publicly held corporation traded on the London Stock Exchange since 1987.

Surface access: Rail — Gatwick Express from London (Victoria) nonstop service every 15 minutes during the day. Connex-South Central from London (Victoria), Clapham Junction, East Croydon, and Brighton. ThamesLink from London Bridge.

Road — Access from the M25 Motorway, via the M23 (junction No 9) via the Gatwick Airport spur road.

Visitor/Photo facilities: Excellent rooftop viewing area at the South Terminal 'Skyview' terrace. (See Other Aviation Attractions, page 89.) Approaching aircraft on Runway 26R can be seen and photographed from South Perimeter Road which can be accessed from steps/lifts in the South Terminal (pedestrians only). Approaching aircraft on Runway 08R can be seen and photographed from Westfield Road, a minor road south from Charlwood village (limited car parking). No good aircraft viewing facilities are available at the North Terminal except from within the flight departure lounge.

Website: www.baa.co.uk

Other information: See listings of useful Gatwick contacts elsewhere in this book.

Gatwick General Information Line — +44 (0)1293 5335353

(This information is believed correct at the time of publication, but should be checked before use.)

World Civil Aircraft Registration Prefixes

Prefix	Country	Prefix	Country	Prefix	Country
AP-	Pakistan	**C2-**	Nauru	**E3-**	Eritrea
A2-	Botswana	**C5-**	Gambia	**F-**	France
A3-	Tonga	**C6-**	Bahamas	**F-O**	France (Outremer)
A40-	Oman	**C9-**	Mozambique	**G-**	United Kingdom
A5-	Bhutan	**D-**	Germany	**HA-**	Hungary
A6-	United Arab Emirates	**DQ-**	Fiji	**HB-**	Switzerland and Liechtenstein
A7-	Qatar	**D2-**	Angola	**HC-**	Ecuador
A9C-	Bahrain	**D4-**	Cape Verde Islands	**HH-**	Haiti
B-	People's Republic of China	**D6-**	Comoro Islands	**HI-**	Dominican Republic
		EC-	Spain	**HK-**	Colombia
B-H	Hong Kong	**EI-**	Ireland	**HL-**	South Korea
B-	Republic of China (Taiwan)	**EK-**	Armenia	**HP-**	Panama
		EL-	Liberia	**HR-**	Honduras
C-	Canada	**EP-**	Iran	**HS-**	Thailand
CC-	Chile	**ER-**	Moldova	**HZ-**	Saudi Arabia
CN-	Morocco	**ES-**	Estonia	**H4-**	Solomon Islands
CP-	Bolivia	**ET-**	Ethiopia	**I-**	Italy
CS-	Portugal	**EW-**	Belarus	**JA-**	Japan
CU-	Cuba	**EX-**	Kyrghystan	**JU-**	Mongolia
CX-	Uruguay	**EY-**	Tajikistan	**JY-**	Jordan
		EZ-	Turkmenistan		

J2-	Djibouti	
J3-	Grenada	
J5-	Guinea-Bissau	
J6-	St Lucia	
J7-	Dominica	
J8-	St Vincent —	
	Grenadines	
LN-	Norway	
LV-	Argentina	
LQ-	Argentina	
LX-	Luxembourg	
LY-	Lithuania	
LZ-	Bulgaria	
N-	United States of	
	America	
OB-	Peru	
OD-	Lebanon	
OE-	Austria	
OH-	Finland	
OK-	Czech Republic	
	(Czechia)	
OM-	Slovakia	
OO-	Belgium	
OY-	Denmark	
P-	Democratic People's	
	Republic of Korea	
PH-	Netherlands	
PJ-	Netherlands Antilles	
PK-	Indonesia	
PP-	Brazil	
PT-	Brazil	
PZ-	Surinam	
P2-	Papua New Guinea	
P4-	Aruba	
RA-	Russia	
RDPL-	Laos	
RP-	Philippines	
SE-	Sweden	
SP-	Poland	
ST-	Sudan	
SU-	Egypt	
SX-	Greece	
S2-	Bangladesh	
S5-	Slovenia	
S7-	Seychelles	
S9-	Sao Tome Island	
TC-	Turkey	
TF-	Iceland	
TG-	Guatemala	

TI-	Costa Rica
TJ-	Cameroon
TL-	Central African
	Republic
TN-	Congo
TR-	Gabon
TS-	Tunisia
TT-	Tchad
TU-	Ivory Coast
TY-	Benin
TZ-	Mali
T3-	Kiribati
T9-	Bosnia
UK-	Uzbekistan
UN-	Kazakhstan
UR-	Ukraine
VH-	Australia
VN	Vietnam
VP-C	Cayman Islands
VP-F	Falkland Islands
VP-L	British Virgin
	Islands
VQ-T	Turks & Caicos
	Islands
VT-	India
V2	Antigua
V3-	Belize
V4-	St Kitts & Nevis
V5-	Namibia
V6-	Micronesia
V7-	Marshall Islands
V8-	Brunei
XA-	Mexico
XB-	Mexico
XC-	Mexico
XT-	Burkina Faso
XU-	Kampuchea
XY-	Myanmar
YA-	Afghanistan
YI-	Iraq
YJ-	Vanuatu
YK-	Syria
YL-	Latvia
YN-	Nicaragua
YR-	Romania
YS-	El Salvador
YU-	Yugoslavia (Serbia
	& Montenegro)
YV-	Venezuela

Z-	Zimbabwe
ZA-	Albania
ZK-	New Zealand
ZP-	Paraguay
ZS-	South Africa
Z3-	Macedonia
3A-	Monaco
3B-	Mauritius
3C-	Equatorial Guinea
3D-	Swaziland
3X-	Guinea
4K-	Azerbaijan
4L-	Georgia
4R-	Sri Lanka
4X-	Israel
5A-	Libya
5B-	Cyprus
5H-	Tanzania
5N-	Nigeria
5R-	Malagasy Republic
5T-	Mauritania
5U-	Niger
5V-	Togo
5W-	Samoa
5X-	Uganda
5Y-	Kenya
6V-	Senegal
6Y-	Jamaica
7O-	Yemen
7P-	Lesotho
7Q-	Malawi
7T-	Algeria
8P-	Barbados
8Q-	Maldive Republic
8R-	Guyana
9A-	Croatia
9G-	Ghana
9H-	Malta
9J-	Zambia
9K-	Kuwait
9L-	Sierra Leone
9M-	Malaysia
9N-	Nepal
9Q-	Democratic Republic
	of Congo
9U-	Burundi
9V-	Singapore
9XR-	Rwanda
9Y-	Trinidad & Tobago

History

Four airports served London in the early 1950s: a fast-developing Heathrow, the over-utilized and unsuitable Blackbushe (west of the Surrey/Hampshire border), the declining and equally unsuitable Croydon, and the all-grass Gatwick. It was the Ministry of Civil Aviation which decided that a more rational approach was required for airports serving the nation's capital. In 1952, the Ministry announced that Gatwick had been chosen from a list of over 50 possible sites, as the location for London's second major airport.

Croydon was being encroached upon by urban development and was too small for the airliners that were then flying. In making their decision, the death writ had also been signed for Blackbushe — in 1959 the Ministry announced the airport was to close for commercial airline traffic, and this it did at midnight on 31 May 1960.

London Heathrow's growth was meteoric following the end of World War 2 and the decision by the government in 1944 disclosed plans to Middlesex County Council for the compulsory purchase of 2,800 acres of land at Heath Row and the old Great West Aerodrome. Heathrow became a civil airport on 1 January 1946 and was officially opened on 31 May the same year. Heathrow's first large terminal (Terminal 2) opened in April 1955 by which time both British Overseas Airways (BOAC) and British European Airways (BEA) were using the airport.

Gatwick was very much in Heathrow's shadow in the early 1950s, but received a huge boost following the Ministry's announcement of its impending development. In fact, it was closed to all commercial traffic in March 1956 at the start of its huge civil engineering programme that cost £7.8 million. The project included extensive drainage, rerouting of a river, the construction of Gatwick's first hard runway, associated taxiways, a new control tower and a state-of-the-art terminal building with boarding 'fingers'. The new building straddled a new railway station on the main London to Brighton railway line and was opened on 27 May 1958. Her Majesty Queen Elizabeth II officially opened the 'new' London Gatwick Airport on 9 June 1958. The *Evening Standard* at the time described

Above: *The Beehive, the former terminal building at Gatwick, built in 1936. It is now a Grade II listed building and was refurbished in late 1999 to become the new headquarters of GB Airways. Geoffrey P. Jones*

Gatwick as 'marvellous', because of its new finger and gate system which enabled passengers to reach their aircraft without walking across windswept aprons or having to catch a bus. It was also claimed to be the first airport in the world to combine air, rail and road transport in a close-knit single unit.

Gatwick's history predates this 1950s development, both historically and in aviation terms. The name Gatwick can be dated back to 1241 when Richard de Warwick assigned his rights to some land — four acres of meadow and 18 acres of other land — in the manor of Charlwood to John de Gatwick and his heirs. This land became part of the Manor of Gatwick and was owned by the de Gatwicks until the 14th century when it was divided amongst several families. A large area of land, which is now to the west of the railway line, was purchased in 1890 by the Gatwick Race Course Company which opened the course the following year with its own railway station. For three years during World War 1, the Aintree Grand National was abandoned and run over the same distance at Gatwick.

Dominion Aircraft Ltd based its Avro 504, G-AACX, at Gatwick from November 1928 but the first regular aviation activity at the site followed the establishment of the Surrey Aero Club. It was founded by Ronald Walters, who obtained the airfield's first licence on 1 August 1930. He quickly obtained his pilot's licence and then acquired several aircraft for his expanding aero club, an Avro 504, an Avro Avian and a de Havilland DH60 Gipsy Moth and, by 1931, an increasing number of affluent racegoers and some jockeys arrived by air for meetings at the adjacent racecourse. The site of the airfield was on low-lying grassland to the east of the threshold of the present Runway 26, extending south through the southern maintenance area to the Beehive terminal site. The bandstand from the old racecourse has been preserved and is now a feature in Crawley town centre.

In 1932, Gatwick Aerodrome was sold to the Redwing Co Ltd. It operated the

Above: *Gatwick Airport in the late 1930s, after the 1936 opening of the circular Beehive terminal. A former Hillman Airways DH86 Express, now in British Airways colours, is parked to the left of the Beehive and in front of the British Airways hangars is one of its Fokker F.XIIs, G-ADZI. In the foreground is the railway line and the ends of the platforms, right.* BAA

Redwing Flying School and the Surrey Aero Club, using examples of the Robinson Redwing two-seat biplane that were manufactured by the Robinson Aircraft Co Ltd at nearby Croydon, before its move in 1932 to new premises at Colchester. The registered office of Redwing Aircraft Ltd moved to Gatwick on 1 July 1932, although aircraft were to be built at Colchester. One of the last aircraft they built, Redwing III G-ABRM, was delivered to Gatwick on 11 May 1933.

Morris Jackaman purchased the aerodrome in 1933 for £13,500 and in 1934 formed Airports Ltd, the same year that the airfield was issued with its first public licence by the Air Ministry, permitting it to be used for scheduled commercial air services for the first time. Airports Ltd secured the services of Marcel Desoutter as business manager and, in 1935, issued 840,000 public shares in its company. Development now proceeded, the airfield was properly drained, the River Mole was diverted and construction of the famous circular Beehive terminal was started. It was completed and officially opened in June 1936 and featured a unique 130m (426ft)-long subway to the new railway station. Designed by architects Hoar, Marlow & Lovett it featured covered canvas awnings that were extended from the main building to the parked aircraft so that passengers could embark and disembark without getting wet if raining. A new railway station serving the airport was opened in September 1935 with Southern Railway trains, running between London (Victoria) and Brighton, stopping there every half-hour. Gatwick was considered to be the most modern airfield, (or perhaps more correctly, airport) of its day.

Hillman Airways was the first airline to operate scheduled services from Gatwick, with flights to Paris and Belfast. In 1935 it became British Airways Ltd (its full name being Allied British Airways) on merging with United Airways and Spartan Airways.

On 17 May 1936, British Airways Ltd switched all its flights from Heston and was now operating services from Gatwick to Paris, Malmo (via Amsterdam), Hamburg, Copenhagen and the Isle of Wight. A single Gatwick to Paris fare cost £4 5s, equivalent today to over £160.00. The mainstay of the British Airways fleet at the time was four ex-Hillman de Havilland DH86 Express airliners. The airline also operated an important night mail service from Gatwick to the Continent. Later, in 1937, British Airways started operating both Lockheed Model 10A Electras (G-AEPN, 'PR and 'SY) and Fokker F.VIIIs (G-AEPT and 'PU) from Gatwick. Fokker F.XII G-AEOS also joined the fleet. Despite all the works to alleviate flooding, the grass airport at Gatwick was still subject to waterlogging and occasional flooding. By 1938, British Airways Ltd, troubled by the interruptions to services by the airport's condition, decided to move its scheduled operations to London's Heston and Croydon airports.

Late in 1936, Capt J. E. Croxon founded Southern Aircraft (Gatwick) Ltd, selling aircraft, carrying out aircraft overhaul and operating charter flights. Dragon Rapides, Percival Proctors and an Avro Anson were used on commercial operations by Southern from both Gatwick and Croydon prior to the war. The company continued to trade after the war but sold its last Rapides in 1952 and, although it flew no more charter flights, Southern Aircraft (Gatwick) operated as an aircraft maintenance company at Gatwick until 1962.

In October 1937 Gatwick Airport also commenced a military career when the 19th Elementary & Reserve Flying Training School was established there using a fleet of DH82A Tiger Moths. This operation continued until September 1939 when the airport was requisitioned by the Air Ministry for use by the Royal Air Force as a satellite to RAF Kenley. It was enlarged with requisitioning of part of the former racecourse. During the war, Gatwick acted as an emergency refuelling station for RAF fighters during the Battle of Britain, was bombed but escaped serious damage. It was also a base for Westland Lysanders, then Curtiss P-40 Tomahawk Is and eventually, North American P-51 Mustangs. Considerable development of hard-standings and aprons took place during the war, but it remained a grass airfield with no hard runway.

Postwar, Gatwick was de-requisitioned and returned to civilian use in 1946. It was used by Airwork Ltd, which carried out maintenance work for the RAF and Royal Navy on Spitfires, Attackers and Sea Hornets. Airwork was also appointed a dealer for the Airspeed Consul and acquired a fleet of DH89 Dragon Rapides and Vickers Vikings, although most of these aircraft operated from its main base at Blackbushe. The Air Ministry designated Gatwick the 'official' London airport for charter companies but there was limited activity on this front as these companies were well entrenched at Blackbushe.

Transcontinental Air Services Ltd was typical of early postwar airlines and was established at Gatwick in 1947 with a single Airspeed AS65 Consul, G-AIOX. Transcontinental flew ad hoc charters from Gatwick to varied destinations in France, Belgium and Switzerland but ceased operations in 1949. Bond Air Services was formed at Gatwick in the summer of 1946, initially flying passenger and freight charters with Auster J/1 G-AGYG and Percival Proctor G-AHMS, but added its first Handley Page Halifax in 1947 for freight charter work. Bond later acquired two DH86Bs for passenger charter work from Gatwick and other southern England airports until the company ceased operations in 1951.

The postwar policy for civil air transport was outlined in the government's white paper, *British Air Transport,* published in March 1945. It proposed three public corporations; BOAC, British South American Airways (BSAA) and BEA. This led to the 1946 Civil Aviation Bill and enabled BEA to begin operations in its own right, serving UK domestic and European destinations. In 1947 the BEA Helicopter Unit was established to explore the potentialities of the helicopter for regular

Above: *Representative of the first scheduled services by BEA from Gatwick to Alderney (Channel Islands) in 1950, a DH89 Dragon Rapide in the airline's colours. This aircraft, G-AGSH, did fly with BEA but is now preserved, flown and owned by Philip Meeson.*
Geoffrey P. Jones

Above: *Former Air Charter Bristol 170 Freighter Mk 32 G-AOUV loading a cargo of racehorses at Gatwick in the mid-1960s. Note the period vehicles and beyond to the left, the hangars and maintenance facilities of British United Airways, and to the right, those of Air Couriers.* Geoffrey P. Jones

scheduled operations and was based at Gatwick, housed at the Beehive terminal building. Bell 47s were used for trials with the GPO (General Post Office) with one trial in the Peterborough-Great Yarmouth area accounting for the collection of 500,000 items of mail by helicopter in the space of four months. Although the world's first scheduled helicopter service between Liverpool and Cardiff started in 1950, it was flown by a BEA, Gatwick-based, Westland-Sikorsky WS55 helicopter. Other 1950s' BEA helicopter experiments included a service between London and Birmingham and from London Heathrow to central London (Waterloo). In 1953, BEA's Gatwick-based helicopters flew to Holland to help with rescue work during the devastating floods. BEA Helicopters Ltd was formed later, in 1964, when two new Sikorsky S61Ns were delivered to Gatwick.

The first service operated by BEA from Gatwick was an experimental twice-weekly scheduled flight to Alderney in the Channel Islands, starting in April 1950. This used Dragon Rapides (G-AHXZ flew the very first flight) and operated in the summer months only. BEA did not have any permanent staff based at Gatwick at

that time so it sent a traffic clerk down from Kensington Air Station to oversee the aircraft's turnround. This service ceased at the end of Summer 1952.

When Her Majesty the Queen officially opened London Gatwick Airport in June 1958 it now had a 2,100m x 46m (7,000ft x 150ft) concrete runway, distinctive high-speed turn-offs to the taxiways, the latest in runway lighting and Calvert-type centreline and bar approach lighting as well as a modern terminal building. The first scheduled service to leave Gatwick on the opening day was BEA DC-3 G-ALXK on a charter flight to Jersey. BEA had already made the decision to transfer its London to Channel Islands flights (Jersey and Guernsey) to the new airport and on the official opening day had scheduled up to seven flights per day to Guernsey and up to 14 to Jersey. By now there were 137 BEA members of staff based at Gatwick. The airport really came into its own in October 1958 when there was thick fog at Heathrow and it handled 98 diverted aircraft movements. Between then and March 1959, Gatwick handled 257 BEA aircraft diverted from Heathrow as well as 230 aircraft of other operators.

Airwork's presence at Gatwick also recommenced in 1958. It took over Transair, an independent airline, which was also based there having recently moved from Croydon. It operated DC-3s on seasonal schedules to Jersey and also flew some of Gatwick's first regular charter flights to destinations such as Alghero, Lourdes, Minorca, Perpignan and Pisa. From 1958, Airwork operated in close association with another independent airline, Hunting-Clan, flying charters from Gatwick, first with Vickers Vikings and then in 1959 with new Vickers V831 Viscounts, these turbo-prop aircraft being used on their 'Blue Nile Viscount' services to Khartoum on behalf of Sudan Airways. On 1 July 1960, Airwork formally merged with associate Hunting-Clan and another independent, Air Charter, to form British United Airways

(BUA). Air Charter's managing director at the time of the merger was Freddie Laker. BUA, with Freddie Laker as its managing director, established its base at Gatwick and built a large hangar and administrative building on the southeastern corner of the airport.

Transair meanwhile was expanding its scheduled colonial coach-class services, its trooping contract with the Ministry of Defence and charter business from Gatwick with the transfer of two Viscounts from Airwork. IT (Inclusive Tour) flights were operated by Transair from Gatwick and the growing list of European destinations served included Bordeaux, Barcelona, Lourdes, Luxembourg, Madrid, Naples, Nice, Palma, Perpignan, Pisa and Toulouse. The number of charter

Right: *Activity at the Air Couriers hangar and apron on Gatwick's south side was extremely varied. Here N2907T, the first Aero Commander 200 seen in the UK, sits outside the main hangar in May 1966. Other aircraft visible include a Dan-Air Ambassador and, behind the tail, a Morton Air Services Dove.* Mike Kemp

Above: *Air Links Canadair C4 Argonauts G-ALHM (left) and G-ALHW were a common sight at Gatwick in the late 1950s and early '60s. Air Links became Transglobe Airways in 1966.* Geoffrey P. Jones

destinations also grew to include Biarritz, Brussels, Copenhagen, Dinard, Geneva, Gothenburg, Le Touquet and Paris (Orly). A Transair Blackpool to Toulouse IT service in the autumn of 1959 frequently stopped off at Gatwick.

The runway soon needed extension with the advent of the first jet airliners and further expansion of the south-side maintenance area also occurred when Air Couriers, formed originally in 1938 at Croydon, moved its aircraft maintenance business there in 1963. Air Couriers also operated a Piper PA23 Apache, G-ARJR, on training and charter flights from Gatwick. In July 1967, the company was taken over by Transglobe Airways, which had been founded at Gatwick as Air Links in 1958 and operated a growing passenger air charter and IT business. Aircraft such as the Handley Page HP81 Hermes and Canadair C4 Argonaut (ferried to nearby Redhill in autumn 1965 prior to their disposal) were flown until the arrival of its first Bristol Britannia aircraft in January 1966, when the change of name to Transglobe took place.

British Independent Airlines Based at Gatwick from 1946

Air Europe — founded in 1978, and expanded rapidly with Boeing 737 and 757s until going bankrupt in March 1991.

Air London — flight training and air taxi company from 1965.

Anglo Cargo Airlines — founded in 1984 to operate non-scheduled Boeing 707 cargo services.

BEA Airtours — subsidiary of BEA formed in 1969 for IT work with Comet 4s and Boeing 707s.

Bond Air Services — air charter (mainly freight) from 1946 to 1951.

British Airtours — originally BEA Airtours, became a charter/IT subsidiary of BA from 1975.

British Caledonian — formed in 1970 with the merger of Caledonian Airways and BUA.

British Island Airways — operated charters and IT flights from 1982 with BAC One-Eleven and MD-83s until 1988.

Cal Air International — IT and group charter DC-10 operator from March 1983, changing its name to Novair International in 1989.

Caledonian Airways — formed in 1961, its first aircraft was an ex-Sabena DC-7C.

Cardinal Airways — formed in 1967, used two DH104 Doves for air taxi and executive charters.

Ciro's Aviation Ltd — operated between 1946 and 1951 flying passenger and freight charters with DC-3s.

Dan-Air — moved from Blackbushe to Gatwick in 1960. Ceased operations in November 1992.

Donaldson International Airways Ltd — between 1964 and 1974 flew Britannias and Boeing 707s.

Eros Airlines — from 1962 flew Vickers Vikings until 1964, the last Viking operator at Gatwick.

Falcon Airways — moved to Gatwick in 1960 flying Hermes, Constellations and a C-54 until 1962.

Hornton Airways — air taxi and charter operator between 1946 and 1950.

Hunting — moved from Luton to Gatwick in 1947, then Bovingdon and Heathrow, but as Hunting-Clan, from Heathrow back to Gatwick in 1960 when it became part of BUA.

IAS Cargo — a Britannia, CL-44 and DC-8 freight airline during the 1970s.

Laker Airways — founded by Freddie Laker in 1966 and revolutionised low-cost air travel, particularly transatlantic with SkyTrain.

Above: *Freddie Laker's ground-breaking DC-10 SkyTrain service from Gatwick to New York was launched on 26 September 1977 after years of negotiations and wrangling with officials, governments and other airlines. A year later, a similar service was started from Gatwick to Los Angeles. Laker Airways ceased operations on 5 February 1982. G-BELO departs Gatwick for New York in May 1981. Geoffrey P. Jones*

Above: *Part of Gatwick's important freight traffic, Tradewinds Boeing 707 G-SAIL, about to roll from Runway 26 in May 1979. Geoffrey P. Jones*

Lloyd International Airways — a DC-4, DC-6, Britannia and Boeing 707 charter airline between 1961 and 1970.

Monarch Airlines — founded in June 1967 by the Cosmos Tours Group at Luton, but a significant user of Gatwick ever since.

Morton Air Services — formed in 1945 and moved from Croydon to Gatwick in 1959. DH Dove, DH Heron and DC-3s flown on scheduled flights and charters until 1968 when the fleet was transferred to BUIA (British United Island Airways).

Orion Airways — founded in 1956 at Blackbushe flying schedules and charters with Vickers Vikings until 1960.

Overseas Aviation — founded in 1957, opened its new hangar at Gatwick in 1960, flew Vikings and Argonauts on charters and IT flights, as well as a Prestwick-Gatwick schedule until bankruptcy in 1961.

Peach Air — flew Boeing 737s and TriStars in 1997, a joint venture between Caledonian Airways and Goldcrest.

Pegasus Airlines — flew Vickers Vikings on IT flights between 1959 and 1961.

Scillonian Air Services — Aero Commander 500 scheduled services between Gatwick and Lands End and Scilly Isles from summer 1963 to October 1964.

Sky Charters — small air taxi and charter airline founded in 1962 used Doves and other small aircraft until 1965.

Southern Aircraft — formed in 1936, flew ad hoc charters with a Rapide and Anson 1946-52. Southern Aircraft (Gatwick) continued aircraft maintenance at Gatwick until 1962.

Swiss Universal — 1960 and '61 flew a Viking on charters from Gatwick, mainly to Basle and Lyon.

Trader Airways — executive jet charter operator founded in 1970 using mainly Falcon 20s until 1974.

Tradewind Airways — took over the CL-44 freighters of Transglobe Airways in 1968 and later Boeing 707s mainly to Africa and the Far East. Ceased operations in January 1986.

Transair — air taxi company founded in 1947 but acquired Consuls and Ansons for freight flights, then DC-3s and Viscounts for scheduled/charter passenger work. Became part of BUA in October 1959.

Trans European Airways — flew Constellation charters from Gatwick from July 1961 until July 1962.

Transglobe Airways — founded as Air Links in 1958, changed name in 1966, acquired CL-44s in 1968 but ceased operations in November 1968 (see Tradewinds above).

Union Air Services — charter airline flying DH86s and a Halifax in 1946 and 1947.

Windmill Theatre Transport Co — private airline using a Rapide flew between 1946 and 1960.

World Wide Aviation — founded 1960, flew C-54 passenger and freight charters until 1962.

During the 1960s, Gatwick was a charter airline paradise. Scheduled services continued, enhanced not only by some of the airlines listed above, but by visiting airlines from the UK, Europe and North America which started to utilize the airport's excellent facilities. Foreign air forces also regularly used Gatwick for transport and liaison flights, particularly the Royal Canadian Air Force. Pacific Western from Canada, Balair and Globeair from Switzerland, Braathens and Wideroes from Norway, Saturn Airways from the USA, Schreiner Air Charters from the Netherlands and Turk Hava Yollari from Turkey were a sprinkling of the airlines that helped Gatwick's traffic growth.

Two additional 'fingers' or piers were constructed from the main terminal building in the early 1960s, the terminal was extended and, by 1964, was handling 1.1 million passengers a year, albeit only the fourth largest airport in Britain behind Heathrow, Manchester and Glasgow. The runway was further extended in 1964 to 2,500m (8,200ft) to enable the airport to handle modern civil airliners such as Boeing 747s and Concordes. By 1967, passenger figures at Gatwick exceeded 2 million per annum for the first time. Further runway extensions took place in 1970 to 2,767m (9,075ft) and in 1973, to 3,099m (10,165ft). British Airports Authority took over the management of Gatwick Airport in 1966.

Right: *Perpignan-based Europe Aero Service Vickers Viking 1B F-BJES (ex-D-BLYK/VP-YHT and G-AJCK) is seen at Gatwick in February 1967, having flown a charter from Paris. Mike Kemp*

Above: *Gatwick in 1965 with corporate Fokker F27 PH-LIP belonging to Dutch radio and electronics company Philips, and to its right alongside the central pier, British United Airways Viscount G-AOXV. Geoffrey P. Jones*

Above: *An aerial view of Gatwick in 1969 showing the three boarding piers radiating from the main terminal building. Some of the first DC-8 jets are seen around the end of the southern pier with Viscounts and BAC One-Elevens with a line up of Britannias to the north. Light aircraft are parked on the grass beyond the central pier. BAA*

Passenger Traffic Growth at Gatwick 1958 to 1998

1958	186,172	**1983**	12,471,300
1963	966,541	**1988**	20,744,000
1968	2,059,535	**1992**	19,670,000
1973	5,728,457	**1998**	29,173,257
1978	7,759,059		

By 1971 there were 60 different airlines regularly using Gatwick. One of the biggest of these was British Caledonian Airways (B.Cal), which started flying transatlantic and South American schedules from there in April 1973, although it had been flying charters to North America for several years prior to this. It was the first British independent airline to operate scheduled flights between London (Gatwick) and New York and had taken over several of the State-owned BOAC's international schedules, as well as those flown by BUA, including to South America and West Africa.

Although based at Luton, Court Line had used Gatwick extensively for holiday charter flights with its fleet of BAC One-Eleven and Lockheed L-1011 TriStars. The collapse of this business in August 1974 affected the whole air charter industry in the UK.

The late 1970s saw Gatwick become the scheduled UK entry airport for two of the big US airlines at the time. Many US charter airlines had already been using the airport and even Delta Air Lines had operated DC-8 charters to Gatwick in the 1960s, but in December 1977, the United States Civil Aeronautics Board awarded the Atlanta-based airline authority to fly scheduled, transatlantic services. Using a Lockheed L-1011 TriStar on lease from TWA, pending delivery of its own TriStar 500s, Delta's first service to Gatwick was on 30 April 1978. Now the world's largest airline in terms of passengers carried, Delta has had a continuous presence at Gatwick ever since. Texas-based Braniff Airways was another scheduled US newcomer to Gatwick soon after, and on 2 June 1980, Minneapolis/St Paul-based Northwest Airlines inaugurated scheduled services from its base and is another of the big US carriers to have served Gatwick continuously ever since.

Above: *Part of British Caledonian's long-haul fleet in 1979, Boeing 707-365C G-ATZC County of Sterling at the airline's south-side maintenance area.* Geoffrey P. Jones

Above: *Braniff's colourful history was matched by its colourful aircraft. Orange-fuselaged Boeing 747-127 N601BN was one of its first Jumbo Jets and inaugurated the Dallas/Fort Worth to London Gatwick schedules in March 1978. Braniff also inaugurated Concorde services between Washington and Dallas/Fort Worth in January 1979 in association with BA and Air France. Geoffrey P. Jones*

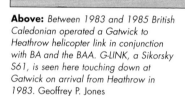

Above: *Between 1983 and 1985 British Caledonian operated a Gatwick to Heathrow helicopter link in conjunction with BA and the BAA. G-LINK, a Sikorsky S61, is seen here touching down at Gatwick on arrival from Heathrow in 1983. Geoffrey P. Jones*

On the domestic front there were several big players at Gatwick in the 1970s offering an increasing number of scheduled services. British Caledonian was flying BAC One-Elevens, competing on routes to Scotland out of Gatwick with those of BEA (which became part of British Airways in 1974) from Heathrow. B.Cal was also flying schedules from Gatwick to Manchester and to Paris and in 1983, in association with British Airways Helicopters and British Airports Authority, introduced a new Gatwick to Heathrow helicopter link using a Sikorsky S61 helicopter (G-LINK), but this was short-lived.

Dan-Air's operation at Gatwick had been centred around the DC-3 and the Airspeed Ambassador in the 1960s but by 1967, its first of two ex-BOAC de Havilland Comet 4s was delivered making the airline only the second independent UK airline to operate jets — BUA was the first. This revolutionised the airline and its ability to serve its growing itinerary of charter destinations. Dan-Air's first BAC One-Elevens were delivered in 1969 and Boeing 707s started to replace the Comets from 1973 but it was not until

November 1980 that the last Dan-Air Comet flight took place, an enthusiasts' charter from Gatwick.

BEA Airtours had been established at Gatwick in April 1969 with a staff of 200 at the airport, mainly recruited from BEA, and was operating surplus BEA Comet 4s. The Helicopter Unit and services to the Channel Islands had until then been the State Corporation's (and subsequently British Airways') only toehold at Gatwick. Its last Comet flight occurred in October 1973, Boeing 707s starting to replace them from December 1971, but this was the real start of the growing dominance of British Airways at Gatwick.

By 1972, Gatwick was ranked the 10th largest airport in Europe and was well in the throes of enlargement and modernisation to handle a planned 8 million passengers by 1975. A new international arrivals hall was opened, the total investment in Gatwick at

Above: *In the 1980s, Dan-Air's Gatwick operations grew phenomenally, including the growth of scheduled services, some flown by the airline's fleet of BAC One-Elevens. G-ATVH, a Srs 207AJ, arrives after a scheduled flight from Newcastle. British Airtours Boeing 737s are seen in the background. Geoffrey P. Jones*

this time being £180 million, and all done without any interruption to the airport's operation. In 1978, Prince Charles formally opened the new and enhanced facilities as the government predicted the growth of the airport to 25 million passengers per annum.

Western Airlines opened a relatively short-lived DC-10 Denver to Gatwick service in May 1981, and in May 1982, American Airlines made its first appearance with the inauguration of a scheduled daily service from Dallas/Fort Worth. A revolutionary new Satellite Pier was opened by Lavinia, Duchess of Norfolk in 1983. This replaced the old north pier or 'finger' and incorporated the first 'Peoplemover' rapid transit system of its kind outside the USA — a total investment of £24 million being involved. Northwest Airlines was one of the first

airlines to move to the Satellite, along with other US airlines, Delta, Air Florida and PEOPLExpress. Also in 1983, approval was given for work to commence on the new North Terminal, and when started it was the largest single civil engineering construction project south of London to have taken place that decade. Charter airlines from the US also began appearing more frequently at Gatwick at this time, including Arrow Air which operated regularly from both Tampa and Miami in Florida with its DC-8-62s and B707-320s.

Right *Western Airlines — which was subsequently taken over by Delta — operated a short-lived Denver to Gatwick scheduled service in 1981; its DC-10-30 N821L* The Londoner *is seen taxying to its parking stand. Geoffrey P. Jones*

Above: *Shortly after the opening of the new Satellite to the South Terminal in 1983, this aerial view shows the wide-body aircraft of Delta, World, Air Florida, CP Air, Pan Am, Northwest Orient and Transamerica, as well as an Olympic Boeing 737.*
Geoffrey P. Jones Collection

Below: *A unique feature of the new Satellite was the 'Peoplemover' Rapid Transit System which connects it with the main South Terminal and is seen here shortly after opening in 1983, with a PEOPLExpress Boeing 747-227B, N602PE, nosed in to the stand that is now most frequently used by Virgin Atlantic. PEOPLExpress was another of the US low-fare airlines that expanded rapidly in the post-1978 Deregulation Act era in the USA.*
Geoffrey P. Jones Collection

The following year, 1984, was very much a landmark in Gatwick's development; handling nearly 14 million passengers, 1.45 million more than in the previous year, it was experiencing a period of phenomenal growth. The growth in passenger numbers was 11.6% despite an increase in aircraft movements of only 3.7%. This emphasises the maximisation of use of Gatwick's single runway and by August Gatwick had exceeded Heathrow in the average number of passengers per aircraft. The greatest increase at Gatwick was represented by scheduled passengers as the airport started its move from a predominantly charter flight airport to a balanced mix of scheduled and charter. The increases were mainly from passengers originating in mainland Europe and the USA, up 21% and 26% respectively over the previous year — charter passengers having increased by only 8%. Gatwick was also handling an increase in cargo traffic as a major new handling facility was completed on the north side of the airport. The cargo tonnage handled at Gatwick in 1984 was 146,300, a 25% increase from the previous year, largely as a result of consolidation and marketing successes by the airport's two resident cargo airlines, Anglo Cargo and Tradewinds. The new air traffic control tower, 45m (148ft) high,

Above: *Delta Air Lines inaugurated its scheduled transatlantic service from Atlanta to Gatwick on 30 April 1978 with Lockheed L-1011 TriStars. It has served Gatwick continuously ever since, the TriStars only being phased out in 1997/98 with the advent of Boeing 767s and in 1999, Boeing 777s. Delta TriStar N752DA is pictured here at Gatwick in 1983.*
Geoffrey P. Jones

was opened, close to the old tower was also opened in 1984.

New services and airlines at Gatwick included Connectair (a B.Cal commuter airline) with schedules to Antwerp and, more significantly, the launch in June 1984 of Virgin Atlantic Airways and its first Boeing 747 schedule from Gatwick to Newark (New York). B.Cal had already commenced scheduled services from Gatwick to Houston, and this received a competitive boost with the inauguration of a daily Continental Airlines Boeing 747 service on the same route. In 1985, another new US airline appeared on schedules at Gatwick, Eastern Air Lines, its DC-10s flying services to Miami.

The original plans for the airport, as announced by the government in the 1950s, provided for a second runway to be added. This proposal had been abandoned in the early 1970s and

Above: *Aircraft at the hold to Runway 08 in 1992 including a Dan-Air Boeing 737-400 and a TWA Boeing 747-200 — the darker area behind the tail of the 737 is the threshold of the combined taxiway and emergency 08 left runway.* Geoffrey P. Jones

Above: *British Airtours Boeing 737-200 G-BGJH, named* Wren, *taxies in company with B.Cal BAC One-Eleven Srs 501 G-AWYR in May 1981.* Geoffrey P. Jones

Gatwick's status as a single-runway airport was reconfirmed by the government in 1985 in a white paper which stated three main points:

- That Gatwick should develop to its full potential as a single-runway airport.

- The government does not support construction of a second runway.

- Proposals for a commuter aircraft runway will not be pursued.

By 1985 however, a modernisation programme saw the completion of refurbishment of the southern pier and the construction of a new emergency runway, which doubled as an additional taxiway and was located between the existing runway and the original taxiway. Gatwick was now handling 42 different scheduled airlines serving 117 destinations in 48 countries. A British Airways Concorde made the type's inaugural visit to Gatwick in July of that year.

The three main resident airlines at Gatwick in the 1980s were British Airways and its charter subsidiary British Airtours, British Caledonian and Dan-Air, as follows:

Airline	Scheduled destinations served	No of scheduled flights per week
BA	15	175 (incl. Airtours)
B.Cal	38	700
Dan-Air	16	116

Under the watchful eye of air traffic control from the new control tower, Gatwick was now handling up to 600 aircraft take-offs and landings per day from its single runway on busy summer weekends. When Virgin Atlantic started its second transatlantic service from Gatwick to Miami in April 1986, it was still a very small airline with just two Boeing 747-200s.

In 1987, BAA, of which Gatwick Airport Ltd is a wholly owned subsidiary, was floated on the London Stock Exchange — 1.35 million people purchasing shares in the company. This was a prelude to the opening in 1988 of the new, £200 million

North Terminal by HM The Queen and the Duke of Edinburgh, which took Gatwick's capacity from 16 million up to 25 million passengers per annum. The North Terminal was linked to the South Terminal by a separate 'Peoplemover' rapid transport system, available free to users of the airport. Other new long-haul airlines which were now using Gatwick included TWA, Transamerica, Aeroflot, Nationair (Canada), Wardair (Canada), Philippine Airlines and Cathay Pacific, as the airport's global status continued to increase. Continental Airlines also increased its presence from 1987 onwards following the takeover of PEOPLExpress, with new services from

Below: *Taken in October 1985, this photograph shows construction work well underway on the new North Terminal. The 'Peoplemover' transit system snakes its way to the South Terminal and the busy Satellite. An Air New Zealand Boeing 747 is also visible at the South Terminal and on the general aviation apron to the right of the construction site are a Viscount, two Bandeirantes and a Jetstream.* Geoffrey P. Jones Collection

Above: When TWA pulled out of Heathrow in 1984 transatlantic flights were transferred to Gatwick; one of its Boeing 767-231ERs, N604TW, is nosed in to the Satellite alongside a Northwest Orient Boeing 747. The North Terminal had not yet been built at this time. Geoffrey P. Jones

Right: Wardair Boeing 747-211B C-GXRD, the fourth 747 to join its fleet, at Gatwick in May 1981. A TAT (France) Fairchild F27 and a Pelican Air Cargo Boeing 707 are parked beyond. Geoffrey P. Jones

Newark (New York), Miami and Denver. Yet another new US airline arrived on the Gatwick scene in June 1987, North Carolina-based Piedmont Airlines with a daily Charlotte Boeing 767-200ER schedule. The Piedmont name disappeared in 1989 following the airline's takeover by USAir, this service continuing until British Airways' alliance with USAir and its adoption of this route. By July 1987 Gatwick had overtaken New York's JFK Airport as the world's second busiest international airport.

The Gulf War and its associated effect on air travel hit the airlines and the airports in the early 1990s. TWA was in crisis and as part of its survival plan agreed to sell American Airlines 12 of its routes, including highly lucrative Heathrow slots. TWA consolidated its remaining transatlantic services at Gatwick, while American was able to consolidate its positions at both Gatwick and Heathrow. American had also taken over the Gatwick-Miami schedule well before Eastern's eventual failure in 1991 and the same year, Pan Am, which had been a Gatwick user, ceased operations due to bankruptcy. A second pier was opened at the North Terminal in 1991, providing an additional 11 pier-served aircraft stands.

British Airtours had continued to expand at Gatwick in the 1980s with a fleet of Boeing 737s and L-1011 TriStars. A new force, in both scheduled and charter services, had also grown up rapidly during this time with Boeing 737s and 757s — Air Europe — a wholly owned subsidiary of the International Leisure Group. Complementing it was a commuter offshoot, Air Europe Express, which had largely taken over the routes of the B.Cal Commuter airline, Connectair, with a fleet of Shorts 360s. Air Europe had been founded at Gatwick in 1978 and started IT flights in May 1979, inaugurating scheduled leisure service flights to Palma in 1985.

British Caledonian Airways had continued to provide extensive scheduled services from Gatwick but was consolidating more and more in the growing leisure market, ordering its first Airbus A320s in 1986. In February 1987, British Airways had been privatised and then merged with B.Cal in the same year — Caledonian Airways continuing to operate under a separate identity as a division of BA until acquired by UK tour operator Inspirations, in December 1994. At the time of the merger a separate charter airline, Cal Air International, had been formed and this changed its name to Novair International Airways in 1989.

When Air Europe Express failed in 1991, several other operators sprang up at Gatwick to take its place. From Belgium, TIA started Swearingen Metroliner schedules to Gatwick from Antwerp and Jersey European Airways took over the Gatwick to Guernsey schedules. Prior to Air Europe Express in the 1980s, these services had been flown by Guernsey Airlines with Viscounts and Shorts 330s. Euroworld Airways was also licensed by the CAA on the Gatwick-Guernsey route, but had soon changed its name to CityFlyer Express, prior to becoming a British Airways franchisee.

The rapidly growing holiday charter market also saw the formation of other specialist airlines, many of whom operated extensive services from Gatwick,

Above: *Pan Am's operations to Gatwick from the USA, and onwards to European destinations, complemented those at Heathrow in 1981. Its fleet of Lockheed L-1011-385 TriStars numbered 12 aircraft including N508PA* Clipper Bald Eagle *seen here at Gatwick in May.* Geoffrey P. Jones

Above: *Guernsey Airlines started as an associate of East Midlands-based Alidair, its first Viscount being G-BDRC. An association with British Air Ferries saw several other Viscounts flown on its scheduled and charter routes, including G-AOYG (pictured) and G-BLOA. The prime service was Guernsey-Gatwick. Geoffrey P. Jones*

Above: *Guernsey Airlines took over the Gatwick to Guernsey schedule in 1981, flying an assortment of types including Shorts 330 and 360s. Its first schedule was from Guernsey to Manchester in April 1980. One of the 330s in the airline's colourful green and white livery is seen on approach to Gatwick's Runway 08 in 1986. Geoffrey P. Jones*

Above: *A trio of Air 2000 Boeing 757-200s in the airline's former colour scheme during the early 1990s. This charter airline commenced services from Manchester in April 1987 as a wholly owned subsidiary of what was then the UK's second largest tour operator, Owners Abroad. Geoffrey P. Jones*

including Manchester-based Air 2000 which had been founded in 1986 and introduced Boeing 757 operations. British Island Airways, abandoning its scheduled services, operated BAC One-Eleven charters and IT flights from its Gatwick base from 1982 onwards. Monarch Airlines, which was founded at Luton in 1967, had a growing base at Gatwick and flew first Boeing 737s, then 757s and Airbus A300-600s. Another expanding Luton-based airline was Britannia Airways — its initial jet fleet of Boeing 737s was supplemented with Boeing 767s and these were regularly flown from Gatwick. Subsequently the 737s were replaced by 757s and these are also a familiar sight at Gatwick. Orion Airways, a subsidiary of Horizon Travel, was established at East Midlands Airport in March 1980, but like Monarch and Britannia, had a considerable presence at Gatwick with its Boeing 737 holiday charter flights.

BAC Charter was also established at Gatwick around 1990 with Twin Otters and an EMB110 Bandeirante, mainly sub-leased to other airlines. Inter European Airways, founded at Cardiff in 1987 with Boeing 737s, started to operate from Gatwick and added Boeing 757s but was subsequently taken over by Airtours. Charter airline Excalibur Airlines started

Above: G-BLKW, a Boeing 767-204, in Britannia Airways' stylish livery at Gatwick in 1986. It had been acquired by this stalwart charter airline in 1985, its fourth 767, the first arriving on the Gatwick scene in 1983. In the mid-1980s, Britannia was carrying 4.5 million passengers annually, a considerable proportion of these passing through Gatwick. Geoffrey P. Jones

operations from East Midlands Airport in May 1992 flying Airbus A320s, but flew most of its charters to Mediterranean destinations from Gatwick. Its existence was short-lived. In 1993/94, Ambassador Airlines flew from Gatwick using Boeing 737s and 757s, but went the same way as Excalibur. Leisure International Airways was an offshoot of Air UK Leisure, both of whom operated at Gatwick with Boeing 737s and 767s, until Leisure's takeover by Air 2000 and the assimilation of its Airbus A321 aircraft into the latter's fleet.

JMC Airlines was formed in 1999, the amalgamation of three British charter airlines, all of which were high profile at Gatwick: Airworld, Flying Colours and Caledonian Airways. The initials JMC are those of the late John Mason Cook, the entrepreneurial son of Thomas Cook. The merger followed the takeover by Flying Colours' tour-operator parent, Thomas Cook, of Caledonian Airways' parent,

Above: *A new airline and colour scheme for 2000 at Gatwick is JMC Airlines, formed from a merger of Airworld, Flying Colours and Caledonian. The fleet is being standardised on the Airbus A320, the Boeing 757-200 — G-JMCA pictured and Boeing 757-300* JMC Airlines

Above: *Former Caledonian Airways DC-10-30 G-GOKT, now in JMC Airlines' colours, is seen at the Satellite, alongside another DC-10 of Northwest Airlines, in February 2000.* Geoffrey P. Jones

Carlson Leisure. The merged airline is linked with German charter airline Hapag-Lloyd through parent company Preussag. All activities were transferred to the JMC banner by March 2000, its Boeing 757s and A320s becoming the workhorses of the airline's 28-aircraft fleet, although retaining ex-Caledonian DC-10s.

A variety of European charter airlines also grace Gatwick's aprons, many of them Spanish. Nortjet started Boeing 737 flights in 1991 and from the embers of Air Europe, Spanish offshoot Air Europa is now flying. Aviaco, which has been using Gatwick for many years, continues to be seen and has been joined by Futura International, Oasis, Meridiana Air, Spanair and Viva Air (Vuelos Internacionales de Vacaciones). The most recent Spanish newcomer, flying schedules with Bombardier/Canadair RJ100s as an Iberia franchisee, is Air Nostrum. Greenair, using Tupolev Tu 154s along with Istanbul Airlines, Pegasus Airlines, Sun Express Air and TUR European Airways, were some of the Turkish-based upstart airlines that used Gatwick from the early 1990s.

African airlines started to use Gatwick, such as Air Zimbabwe, first with Boeing 707s and then with its Boeing 767-200ERs. Cameroon Airlines with Boeing 707s, Ghana Airways using DC-10s, Okada Air (Nigeria) with BAC One-Elevens, and Uganda Airlines with Boeing 707s could also all be seen. Air New Zealand, Cathay Pacific and Eva Air (Taiwan) also used Gatwick prior to acquiring rights to fly to Heathrow. Nationair was a regular, along with several other Canadian airlines including Canadian Airlines International and Air Transat. Austrian Airlines, Olympic (Greece) and Cyprus Airlines were all using Gatwick and in March 1992 the French regional airline TAT European Airlines started flying scheduled services from Paris (Charles de Gaulle) using Fokker 100s. As an expansion of the Virgin name, Greek airline South East European Airlines, started flying schedules to Athens in 1993 under the Virgin banner. More recently, Brussels-based, low-fare airline Virgin Express has introduced services linking Gatwick with its European hub at Brussels.

Above: *Nortjet Boeing 737-400 EC-EMI, one of four in this Spanish charter operator's fleet which flew from Gatwick to both the Balearic and Canary Islands. It was formed in 1987 as Euskal Air.* Geoffrey P. Jones

Below: *Meridiana was originally the Sardinian-based airline Alisarda, but adopted its new name in 1991. It started scheduled services to Gatwick using this BAe146, I-FLRV, between both Pisa and Florence and continues to serve the airport but now uses mainly McDonnell Douglas MD-80s.* Geoffrey P. Jones

Above: *Formed in 1988 by Iberia and Lufthansa, Vuelos Internacionales de Vacaciones, or Viva Air for short, flew services from Gatwick with Boeing 737-300s (EC-FER pictured in March 1992) to Barcelona, Madrid and Malaga. Geoffrey P. Jones*

Right: *Greenair was one of many upstart Turkish airlines that commenced operations in the 1990s and flew charters from Gatwick to Turkish Mediterranean resorts. Services were flown in 1992 with this Tupolev Tu-154, TC-GRB. Geoffrey P. Jones*

Below: *Air Zimbabwe has been a regular user of Gatwick since 1980. Here, Boeing 707-330B VP-WKS is seen in May 1981 as construction of the new Satellite gets underway. Geoffrey P. Jones*

Left: *Okada Air of Nigeria was founded in 1983 to operate domestic and international passenger charter flights. BAC One-Eleven Srs 420EL, 5N-ADS, ex-C-GQBV, was an unusual visitor to Gatwick on 2 November 1985.* Geoffrey P. Jones

Above: *Hong Kong-based Cathay Pacific flew services to London Gatwick from the late 1970s until transferring to Heathrow in the mid-1990s. Boeing 747-200 VR-HKG is seen here in 1981.* Geoffrey P. Jones

The new North Terminal international departures lounge was opened in 1994, almost simultaneously with similar facilities in the new South Terminal. By 1998, there were over 102 airlines flying from Gatwick to over 280 international destinations and accounting for 251,321 departures per annum. The importance of the airport to the local Horley and Crawley economies and also much further afield in southeast England, can be gauged by the fact that over 27,000 people are employed there. Gatwick's international status is now huge, the airport's scheduled network including direct services to over

22 cities in the USA, more than from any other European airport, including Heathrow.

Some of the recent newcomers to the Gatwick airline scene include Maersk Air with 36 flights weekly linking with Copenhagen, Billund and Kristiansand. Also, Alitalia is now well established on its services to Rome and Pisa, as are Ryanair, GB Airlines (as a BA franchisee) and LOT (Poland) flying to Gdansk, Ukraine International, Croatia Airlines, Transavia, and many others. Gatwick also sees the downside of the difficult trading environment of many newer airlines.

Above: *Eva Air's rapid worldwide expansion, following the airline's formation in July 1991, included a service to Gatwick from 1993 when its Boeing 767-300ERs started twice-weekly flights from Taipei (Taiwan). B-16603 is pictured at the Satellite in April 1993. Eva Air is a subsidiary of Taiwan's Evergreen Group, the world's largest container shipping line, but has now moved its London service to Heathrow. Geoffrey P. Jones*

Above: *TAT European Airlines started scheduled services to Gatwick from Paris Charles de Gaulle in March 1992 using Fokker 100s, including F-GIOV. This airline was subsequently taken over by BA. Geoffrey P. Jones*

Below: *One of the last BAC One-Eleven operators at Gatwick was AB Airlines, until it ceased trading in 1999. Its BAC One-Eleven Srs 510ED, G-AVMW, was one of two ex-British Airways aircraft in the fleet, along with three leased Boeing 737-300s (sub-leased to other airlines). These were used for schedules from Gatwick to Shannon, Nice, Lisbon and Berlin and also for charter flights. AB had ordered six new Boeing 737-700s and cited their late delivery as one of the reasons for its demise. Geoffrey P. Jones*

AB Airlines, which had been a growing user of Gatwick with its BAC One-Elevens and Boeing 737s on services to Shannon, Lisbon and Berlin was one of 1999's casualties, a reminder of the darker days of Air Europe and Dan-Air.

British Airways' dominance at Gatwick was further enforced in 1998 with the decision to introduce Boeing 777s on services from the airport and to base a substantial proportion of this fleet there. This was part of a plan to develop more long-haul destinations from Gatwick, many of these destinations being moved from Heathrow. Along with franchisees, CityFlyer Express, Brymon, Air Liberté, Deutsche BA and GB Airways, BA's range of domestic, European and worldwide flights from Gatwick is now bigger than ever. (See separate section on BA at Gatwick.)

Gatwick is now the seventh busiest international airport in the world, a major achievement for a single-runway facility. In the first three months of 1999, the Airports Council International ranked Gatwick the 29th-largest airport in the world by the number of passengers and it was ranked the sixth fastest growing with an annual growth rate of 9.5%. It can schedule up to 48 flights per hour (either a take-off or a landing) from its runway and on the busiest day in 1998, Sunday 16 August, it handled 122,181 passengers. The peak time was the week ending Saturday 5 September with 762,576 passengers handled. The top 10 destinations from Gatwick in 1998 were:

City/Country	No of passengers
Malaga, Spain	897,568
Palma, Majorca	703,340
Orlando, Florida, USA	702,269
Tenerife, Canary Islands	700,734
Faro, Portugal	608,606
Dublin, Republic of Ireland	584,381
Newark (New York), USA	486,580
Alicante, Spain	476,580
Atlanta, Georgia, USA	468,596
Houston, Texas, USA	466,004

Below: With most stands occupied, Gatwick's South Terminal and the Satellite contribute to a summer total daily throughput of passengers of over 120,000. Geoffrey P. Jones

BAA's future development strategy for Gatwick focuses on expansion as a single-runway, two-terminal airport to handle around 40 million passengers per annum by 2008. These projections are based on higher passenger traffic forecasts for southeast England and the decision by BA to establish and develop a hub operation at the airport. However, given the poor BA financial results for 1999, its citing of its passenger yields at Gatwick as being too low (its costs are only marginally lower than at Heathrow), and the continuing heavy losses of its French and German franchisees, Air Liberté and Deutsche BA, such a growth figure may yet prove to be over-optimistic. Nonetheless, BAA Gatwick plans to invest between £80 and £100 million a year over the next five years to expand both the North and South Terminals incrementally to meet passenger and business requirements. A 7,500sq m (80,625sq ft) extension to the South Terminal international departure lounge to provide more seating, shops, restaurants and lounge facilities and a new flight connections centre was scheduled for completion in early 2000.

Gatwick's role as a joint business and leisure departure airport is emphasised by Aer Lingus's move of its Dublin services to Gatwick in January 2000 from Stansted. This is part of the airline's plan to increase its capacity in the London market by 11%, with the aim of adding further services from Gatwick to both Cork and Shannon in April of 2001. Aer Lingus views Stansted mainly as a leisure-orientated airport and expects to handle more business traffic through Gatwick as a result of the move. It could also reflect Aer Lingus's plan to become a member of the **one**world™ airline alliance, headed by BA and American, both of whom already have a strong presence at Gatwick.

The Civil Aviation Authority (CAA) estimates that during the summer season of 1999 over 50% of all charter flights from Gatwick (and Manchester) were delayed. This was because of problems with European air traffic control delays and slot constraints at the major airports. It was also due to the re-routing effects of the Balkan war. The worst affected charter destinations were Corfu, Alicante and Palma.

Airfield concepts published by BAA Gatwick saw the 1999 completion of eight remote Boeing 747 stands to the west of the control tower. It also intends to provide a further pier or satellite service for the northwest zone of the airport, linked to the North Terminal. Currently, 70-75% of passengers using the North Terminal receive pier service whereas BAA's agreed service standard is 90-95%. The development strategy will also make provision for improved cargo handling, aircraft maintenance, car parking and other necessary airport facilities.

1999 — Another Record Year at Gatwick

Continuing the trend from 1998, Gatwick airport's traffic has continued to grow (see figures on page 19). The total number of passengers using the airport in 1999 was up 4.7% on 1998's figure, at 30.41 million — this is split between 27.63 million international passengers (up 5%) and 2.78 million domestic passengers (up 1.6%). The cargo tonnage handled by the airport in 1999 totalled 313,600, of which 295,000 tonnes was cargo and the rest mail. The passengers and cargo were flown on a total of 246,500 commercial flights — a tiny number of general aviation and 'other' flights were also handled when compared to the 'commercial' total. Gatwick handled 255,539 take-offs and landings.

Gatwick's performance is part of the improved BAA's figures overall for its seven UK airports, which reached a record 116.9 million passengers in 1999, a 5.7% increase over 1998. Gatwick can be compared to the two other main

London airports, Heathrow which handled 62 million passengers in 1999, a 2.7% increase over the previous year and Stansted, which handled 9.4 million passengers, a 38% increase. Gatwick's figure is ascribed to increases on European scheduled flights, North Atlantic and other long-haul and Irish routes.

The busiest day at Gatwick in 1999 was Saturday 7 August when 126,619 passengers were handled and the peak week's traffic was 17-23 August with 798,075 passengers. The top 10 destinations from Gatwick changed slightly from those in 1998 as follows:

1999 Ranking	City/Country	No of Passengers	1998 Ranking
1	Orlando	925,536	3
2	Malaga	845,149	1
3	Palma, Majorca	756,152	2
4	Tenerife, Canary Islands	715,152	4
5	Dublin, Ireland	619,684	6
6	Faro, Portugal	599,673	5
7	Alicante, Spain	518,371	8
8	Atlanta, USA	506,265	9
9	Newark, USA	492,070	7
10	Amsterdam, Holland	466,679	-

In a rapidly changing airline world the services offered to and from Gatwick are in a constant state of flux. Some of the more recent changes at the end of 1999 and beginning of 2000 include:

- Aer Lingus started its Dublin to Gatwick schedules in January 2000 flying Boeing 737-500s and hoped to start services from both Cork and Shannon to Gatwick later in the year.

- easyJet Switzerland started its Zurich to Gatwick schedules in January 2000.

- Virgin Atlantic has acquired two more ex-Air New Zealand Boeing 747-200 'Classics' — G-VSSS, delivered in February, followed by G-VPUF in May 2000.

- Virgin Sun will add an Airbus A321 to its A320 fleet during the summer season of 2000.

- TAP Air Portugal restarted services to Gatwick on 6 February 2000 with a daily Lisbon to Gatwick flight, except on Saturdays.

- GB Airways launched a Gatwick to Nantes (France) schedule with Boeing 737s on 9 March 2000, competing with Air France/Brit Air and its Bombardier CRJ-100s. GB is also looking to take over some of BA's less profitable routes out of Gatwick and to expand its services to outside its present western Mediterranean service area. GB Airways has also ordered Airbus A320s.

- Sabre Airways is to acquire more Boeing 737-800s and two more Boeing 727s which will be retrofitted with BF Goodrich 'super 27' modifications to make them 36% quieter.

- BA is to launch a three-times-a-week Boeing 767 service from Gatwick to Abuja/Port Harcourt (Nigeria). It plans to withdraw from its Gatwick to Moscow schedules to concentrate on its Heathrow to Moscow twice daily schedule.

- British World Airlines are to launch charter flights from Gatwick to Cyprus, Greece, Spain and Turkey from May 2000 onwards using its newly delivered Boeing 737-300.

The Future

BAA Gatwick has stated vehemently that it has no plans for a second runway at Gatwick. In fact, there is a legally binding agreement with West Sussex-County Council that prevents the construction or opening of another runway before the year 2019. In the early 1990s the government commissioned the RUCATSE (Runway Capacity to Serve the South East) study to look at the future growth of the three main London airports, Heathrow, Gatwick and Stansted. In February 1995, the government rejected the study's notional scheme for a second runway at Gatwick. The government then asked BAA to examine whether there might be a less environmentally damaging option, such as a close parallel runway at Gatwick. However, in January 1998 BAA asked the government to put the study on hold. It is strictly a matter for the government to decide whether additional runway capacity should ever be proposed somewhere in the South East. In March 1999, the government announced its intention to undertake a further series of studies into airport capacity, looking 30 years ahead and this is expected to take about two years to complete. BAA's stated priority policy at Gatwick is to make best use of its one runway and two terminals.

Governments change as do policies, however, and applications are believed to have been made already for additional maintenance hangars on the northern perimeter of the airport, albeit they were rejected. Some speculators believe that if the economic climate is right, these applications could be revived and approved. This would free up the current huge maintenance area on the southern perimeter of the airport for expansion, possibly with the much sought-after Gatwick commuter runway. Time will tell, but BAA's stated aim is to take its responsibilities as a neighbour very seriously, with any developments requiring planning permissions, which would be prepared in full consultation with the local authorities, neighbours and customers.

Above: *Wearing the new Delta Air Lines livery first introduced in 1997, Boeing 767-300ER N153DL (ex-A40-GM) is serviced by Gatwick Handling at a remote parking stand. It will be moved to a gate at the North Terminal for passenger boarding prior to its early afternoon departure to Atlanta. Geoffrey P. Jones*

Above: *Boeing 767-200ERs of US Airways and TWA at the holding points for Runway 26 prior to their clearances to line up and depart for Charlotte, North Carolina and St Louis, Missouri respectively. The 'Welcome to Gatwick' sign on the roof of the South Terminal is now far less prominent than before, following the 1999 building expansion which was still underway in this November view. Geoffrey P. Jones*

Above: *With 42 DC-10s, Northwest Airlines currently has the largest operational fleet in the world of passenger-carrying aircraft of the type. The fleet includes both the General Electric GE CF6-50C-powered DC-10-30 and the Pratt & Whitney JT-9D-20-powered DC-10-40. N234NW, a DC-10-30, taxies towards its stand at the Satellite in November 1999. Northwest made application in early 2000 to the US Department of Transport for clearance to operate its services from Minneapolis/St Paul and Detroit to Heathrow in anticipation of the latest US/UK bilateral negotiations. Geoffrey P. Jones*

Gatwick is now well established as the world's sixth busiest international airport and the 21st-busiest in terms of domestic passenger traffic. At the end of 1999, Gatwick traffic levels were up 2.6% overall, the most significant growth areas being 6.4% on the North Atlantic, 7.9% on the Channel Islands and 6.7% on other long-haul services. Domestic traffic growth at Gatwick is described as 'flat' despite a general transfer of domestic traffic and routes from Heathrow. Gatwick is handling over 3.1 million passengers per month (compared with 5.6 million at Heathrow), this accounting for 22,700 air transport movements per month (38,200 movements at Heathrow).

British Airways' acquisition of CityFlyer Express will have far-reaching effects. When Dan-Air's schedules were taken over by BA, its Euro-Gatwick operation was established, but kept separate from BA's mainline operation. Many sub-800km (500 mile) routes from Gatwick, both domestic and European, are likely to be taken away from BA mainline and transferred to CityFlyer — these representing 35% of BA's services. With the switch, some of BA's Boeing 737s could also be transferred to CityFlyer and its fleet of Avro RJ100s could be boosted. However, considerable staff restructuring will have to be dealt with to achieve this shift, and with operating losses for BA predicted at year end on 31 March 2000, a large cut in its Gatwick workforce could also occur.

Gatwick's big US airlines, Delta, Northwest, US Airways (previously USAir) and Continental, would all like to operate at least some of their transatlantic services into Heathrow, not wholly forsaking Gatwick, but perhaps diversifying to both airports as American Airlines has done. In January 2000, Northwest Airlines announced it had applied to the US Department of Transport for clearance to operate services between Heathrow and its Detroit and Minneapolis/St Paul hubs. This move is a direct result of the airline's anticipation of the outcome of the latest UK-US bilateral negotiations, and the perception that limited access may be agreed for US operators at Heathrow.

In the rapidly changing world of air transport, Gatwick Airport sees more than its fair share of upstarts, failures and changes. There is no reason at all to believe this will be different in the 21st century, some of the recently taken photographs of airlines and airliners illustrating this book becoming just historical memories when these pages are thumbed in a few years time.

Below: *Continental was the first overseas airline to introduce Boeing 777 services to Gatwick. One of its daily Gatwick-Houston schedules, departing mid-morning, is now flown by a 777-224ER. N78001 pushes back at departure from its stand at the South Terminal in April 1999. Geoffrey P. Jones*

British Airports Authority (BAA)

BAA is the world's largest commercial operator of airports. It owns and operates seven airports in the UK, at Heathrow, Gatwick, Stansted, Glasgow, Edinburgh, Aberdeen and Southampton. Outside the UK it manages all or part of eight airports, at Pittsburgh, Indianapolis, Harrisburg and Newark (New York) in the USA, Melbourne and Launceston in Australia, Naples in Italy, and Mauritius. It serves more than 178 million passengers per annum worldwide, of which 112.5 million are in the UK. All seven of BAA's UK airports reached all time high passenger volumes in 1998/99 and all its major airports grew steadily, with North Atlantic services topping the growth at 9.5%. BAA continues to invest in new and improved facilities to meet increasing demand, investing £512 million in airport facilities in 1998/9.

BAA claims to be the world's largest 'travel retail specialist', with several hundred shops and other retail outlets

Above: *Having proceeded through security and into the departure lounge of the South Terminal, passengers find a large range of tax-free shops, restaurants and food outlets to cater for their needs prior to boarding their aircraft. Geoffrey P. Jones*

and concessions at its airports, other airports in the USA, on the US borders with Canada and Mexico, on board the aircraft of 28 airlines, and at either end of the Channel Tunnel. At Gatwick BAA's retail revenue for 1998/99 was £199 million, representing a 7.4% growth on the previous year. The transfer of duty-free contracts to World Duty Free Europe Ltd continued during 1998/99 following the new EU directive on the abolition of duty-free. BAA believes the abolition of European duty-free sales could have affected its profits by as much as £80 million in 1999.

In 1998/9 the revenue earned by BAA totalled £2,013 million of which by far the largest proportion, £1,292 million, was from its UK and international airports. However, throughout BAA the largest individual source of revenue was from retail activities at £1,033 million. Its revenue from airport and other traffic charges was just over half this figure, at £574 million.

BAA also prides itself on the level of its airport landing charges, London Gatwick in particular being one of the lowest of major European airports, and ranked 20th in 1998/99. These are the charges made to airlines for landing, parking, etc and have fallen in real terms by at least 15% in the last 10 years.

Major investment by BAA continues at Gatwick, the latest development being the £30 million plan at the North Terminal for a 6,455sq m (69,456sq ft) extension to offer 70% more seating and more catering and shopping services for its customers. This work is scheduled to be completed by November 2001.

Below: *Britannia Airways Boeing 757-200 G-OAHF has an airbridge in place as Emirates Airbus A310-304 A6-EKD waits at the hold for Runway 26. Emirates is the international airline of the United Arab Emirates and was founded by the government of Dubai in May 1985. In the background is a BA DC-10 at the British Airways Engineering facility on the airport's south side. Geoffrey P. Jones*

Responsibilities for BAA and Air Travel Operations at Gatwick and Other BAA Airports

BAA

- All airport facilities — including electricity, heating, lighting, water, sewerage, fire alarms
- Car parks
- Security at airports
- Passenger security screening
- Shops and other commercial services such as catering, car hire and bureaux de change
- Flight information display systems
- Information desks/points
- Air bridges
- Airport fire services
- Runways/taxiways/aprons

Airlines
- Checking-in passengers and allocating seats
- Cargo
- Baggage handling
- Manoeuvring airbridge to aircraft
- Pushing back aircraft
- Loading luggage on to aircraft
- Boarding passengers and operating gate

(Air traffic control is the responsibility of the Civil Aviation Authority.)

Above: *Air Zimbabwe Boeing 767-200ER Z-WPF is handled by Gatwick Handling during turnround after its daily, early morning arrival from Harare, in April 1999.* Geoffrey P. Jones

Airlines Flying Scheduled Services from Gatwick (Correct to January 2000)

Airline	ICAO three-letter designator	Airline two-letter designator	South/North Terminal
AB Airlines (ceased 10/99)	AZX	7L	S
Aer Lingus	EIN	EI	S
Aeroflot — Russian International	AFL	SU	S
Air Europa	AEA	UX	S
Air France	AFR	AF	S
Air Gabon	AGN	GN	S
Air Malta	AMC	KM	S
Air Seychelles	SEY	HM	S
Air Zimbabwe	AZW	UM	S
Air 2000	AMM	DP	N
Alitalia	AZA	AZ	S
American Airlines	AAL	AA	S
Azerbaijan Airlines	AHY	J2	S
Base Airlines	BRO	5E	S
(Business Aviation Service Eindhoven)	(BA)		
Belavia Belarussian Airlines	BLI		S
British Airways	BAW	BA	N
Brymon Airways (operated by BA)	BRY	BC	N
Cameroon Airlines	UYC	UY	S
Channel Express (Freight/Mail)	EXS	LS	-
Continental Airlines	COA	CO	S
CityFlyer Express	CFE	FD	S
Croatia Airlines	CTN	OU	S

Airline	ICAO three-letter designator	Airline two-letter designator	South/North Terminal
Cubana	CUB	CU	S
Cyprus Airways	CYP	CY	S
Debonair	DEB	2G	S
Delta Air Lines	DAL	DL	N
Deutsche BA (operated by BA)	BAG	DI	N
EasyJet Airlines	EZY	U2	S
Emirates	UAE	EK	N
Estonian Air	ELL	OV	S
European Regional Airlines	EUA	EA	S
Finnair	FIN	AY	S
Futura Direct	FUA	FH	S
Garuda Indonesia	GIA	GA	S
GB Airways (operated by BA)	GBL	GT	N
Jersey European Airways	JEA	JY	S
Iberia (Air Nostrum)	IBE	IB	S
Lauda Air	LDA	NG	N
LOT Polish Airlines	LOT	LO	N
Maersk Air	DAN	DM	N
Malev Hungarian Airlines	MAH	MA	S
Meridiana	ISS	IG	S
Northwest Airlines	NWA	NW	S
Royal Nepal Airlines	RNA	RA	N
Ryanair	RYR	FR	S
Spanair	JKK	JK	S
TAT/Air Liberté (operated by BA)	LIB	IJ	N
Transavia	TRA	HV	S
Trans Brasil	TBA	TR	S
Trans World Airlines	TWA	TW	S
Ukraine International Airlines	AUI	PS	S
US Airways	USA	US	S
Virgin Atlantic Airways	VIR	VS	S
Yemenia	IYE	IY	S

Right: *Operating Aeroflot's scheduled flights from Leningrad to London Gatwick in the autumn of 1985 were the first Ilyushin Il86s to be seen in the UK. CCCP-86065 is shown here taxying for take-off on Runway 26. Take-off is characterised by the high-pitched and extremely noisy whining of its Kuznetsov turbofan jet engines. Geoffrey P. Jones*

Above: *Formed by former Formula One motor racing driver Niki Lauda in 1987 as an air taxi/charter airline, Lauda Air has subsequently diversified and operates scheduled flights worldwide. Its Salzburg and Vienna flights are flown by either Bombardier/Canadair RJ100s such as OE-LRD illustrated, or Boeing 737-300s and uses the South Terminal.* Geoffrey P. Jones

Above: *Following the break up of the Soviet Union, many airlines from the newly independent states were formed. One of these, Ukraine International Airlines, flies services to Gatwick from Kiev using this former Taiwanese Boeing 737-2T4, UR-GAD. Its small fleet also includes Boeing 737-300s.* Geoffrey P. Jones

Non-Scheduled Airlines Using
Gatwick Regularly (Correct to October 1999)

Airline	ICAO 3-letter designator	Airline 2-letter designator	Handling Agent*
Canada			
Air Transat	TSC	TS	GHI
Canada 3000 Airlines	CMM	2T	GHI
Canadian Airlines	CDN	CP	
Royal Aviation	ROY	QN	SVR
United Kingdom			
Airtours International Airways	AIH	VZ	SVR
Britannia Airways	BAL	BY	SVR
British Midland	BMA	BD	SVR
British World Airlines	BWL	VF	SVR
Caledonian Airways (see JMC)	CKT		GHI
European Air Charter	EAF		GHI
Flightline/Palmair	FLT		
Flying Colours (see JMC)	FCL	SVR	
Interflight	IFT		
JMC Airlines	JMC	MT	GHI
Monarch Airlines	MON	ZB	BMH
Sabre Airways	SBE	Z6	SVR
Virgin Sun	VIR		BMH

Below: *Airtours operate a variety of Airbus types on medium- and long-haul holiday charter flights from Gatwick. G-COEZ is one of its A320-231s. Airtours now uses the radio call sign prefix 'Kestrel' on all radio transmissions. Geoffrey P. Jones*

Above: *One of the first Airbus A330 operators at Gatwick was Monarch Airlines. Its first of two A330-242s, G-EOMA, was delivered in April 1999 and is seen here taxying out for departure in July of that year. Geoffrey P. Jones*

Airline	ICAO 3-letter designator	Airline 2-letter designator	Handling Agent*
United States of America			
American Trans Air	AMT	TZ	SVR
Sun Country Airlines	SCX	SY	
World Airways	WOA	WO	
Other Countries			
AOM French Airlines, France	AOM	IW	SVR
Air Alfa, Turkey	AFA	H7	SVR
Air Algérie, Algeria	DAH	AH	GHI
Arkia, Israel	AIZ	IZ	SVR
Balkan Bulgarian, Bulgaria	LAZ	LZ	SVR
El Al, Israel	ELY	LY	SVR
Eurocypria, Cyprus	ECA	UI	SVR
Istanbul Airlines, Turkey	IST	IL	GHI
Nouvelair Tunisie, Tunisia	LBT	BJ	SVR
Novair, Sweden	NVR	1I	SVR
Onur Air, Turkey	OHY	8Q	SVR
Pegasus Airlines, Turkey	PGT		SVR
Royal Jordanian, Jordan	RJA	RJ	SVR
SATA — Air Acores, Azores	RZO	S4	SVR
Top Air, Turkey	TOP	B6	SVR
Transaer International, Ireland	TLA	T7	GHI
Via Bulgarian Airways, Bulgaria	VIM	VL	SVR

Scheduled Destinations Served
(Generally, direct flights only)

City/Country	Airline	North or South Terminal	Handling agent*
Aberdeen, UK	British Airways	N	BA
Abidjan, Cote d'Ivoire	British Airways	N	BA
Abuja, Nigeria	British Airways	N	BA
Accra, Ghana	British Airways	N	BA
Alicante, Spain	GB Airways (BA)	N	BA
	Iberia	S	SVR
Almaty, Kazakhstan	British Airways	N	BA
Amsterdam, Netherlands	CityFlyer Express (BA)	S	BMH
	KLM‡	S	SVR
	‡likely to withdraw services in spring 2000		
	Transavia	S	SVR
Antigua, Leeward Islands	British Airways	N	BA
	Virgin Atlantic	S	BMH
Antwerp, Belgium	CityFlyer Express (BA)	S	BMH
Athens, Greece	British Airways	N	BA
	Virgin Atlantic	S	BMH
Atlanta, USA	British Airways	N	BA
	Delta Air Lines	N	GHI
Baku, Azerbaijan	Azerbaijan Airways	S	SVR
	British Airways	N	BA
Baltimore, USA	British Airways	N	BA
Bangkok, Thailand	Garuda Indonesia	S	GHI
Barcelona, Spain	Air Europa	S	GHI
	British Airways	N	BA
Belfast, UK	Jersey European Airways	S	SVR
Belgrade, Yugoslavia	British Airways	N	BA
Bermuda	British Airways	N	BA
Billund, Denmark	Maersk Air	N	GHI
Bogota, Colombia	British Airways	N	BA
Bologna, Italy	Alitalia	S	SVR
Bordeaux, France	Air Liberté (BA)	N	BA
Boston, USA	American Airlines	S	SVR
	Virgin Atlantic	S	BMH
Bremen, Germany	CityFlyer Express (BA)	S	BMH
Brest, France	BritAir/Air France	N	GHI
Bridgetown, Barbados	British Airways	N	BA
	Virgin Atlantic	S	BMH
Bristol, UK	Brymon Airways (BA)	N	BA
Brussels, Belgium	British Airways	N	BA
	Sabena	S	
	Virgin Express	S	BMH

City/Country	Airline	North or South Terminal	Handling agent*
Bucharest, Romania	British Airways	N	BA
Budapest, Hungary	Malev	N	BA
Buenos Aires, Argentina	British Airways	N	BA
Caen, France	BritAir/Air France	N	GHI
Cancun, Mexico	British Airways	N	BA
Caracas, Venezuela	British Airways	N	BA
Casablanca, Morocco	GB Airways (BA)	N	BA
Cayo Lago del Sur, Cuba	Cubana	S	GHI
Charlotte, USA	British Airways	N	BA
	US Airways	S	GHI
Cincinnati, USA	Delta Air Lines	N	GHI
Cleveland, USA	Continental Airlines	S	SVR
Cologne, Germany	CityFlyer Express (BA)	S	BMH
Copenhagen, Denmark	Maersk Air	N	GHI
Cork, Republic of Ireland	CityFlyer Express (BA)	S	BMH
Dallas/Fort Worth, USA	American Airlines	S	SVR
	British Airways	N	BA
Dar es Salaam, Tanzania	British Airways	N	BA
Denpasar Bali, Indonesia	Garuda Indonesia	S	GHI
Denver, USA	British Airways	N	BA
Detroit, USA	Northwest Airlines	S	GHI
Dhahran, Saudi Arabia	British Airways	N	BA
Douala, Cameroon	Cameroon Airlines	S	SVR
Dubai, UAE	Air Seychelles	S	GHI
	Emirates	N	GHI
	Royal Nepal Airlines	N	BA
Dublin, Republic of Ireland	Aer Lingus	S	
	CityFlyer Express (BA)	S	BMH
	Ryan Air	S	SVR
Düsseldorf, Germany	CityFlyer Express	S	BMH
Edinburgh, UK	British Airways	N	BA
Eindhoven, Netherlands	Base Airlines (BA)	S	BA
Entebbe/Kampala, Uganda	British Airways	N	BA
Faro, Portugal	GB Airways (BA)	N	BA
Florence, Italy	British Airways	N	BA
	Meridiana	S	SVR
Frankfurt, Germany	Air Zimbabwe	S	GHI
	British Airways	N	BA
	Deutsche BA	N	BA
	Royal Nepal Airlines	N	BA
Funchal, Madeira	GB Airways (BA)	N	BA
Gdansk, Poland	British Airways	N	BA
Geneva, Switzerland	British Airways	N	BA
	easyJet	S	
Genoa, Italy	British Airways	N	BA
Gibraltar	GB Airways (BA)	N	BA

City/Country	Airline	North or South Terminal	Handling agent*
Glasgow, UK	British Airways	N	BA
Gothenburg, Sweden	British Airways	N	BA
Grand Cayman Island	British Airways	N	BA
Grenada, Windward Islands	British Airways	N	BA
Guernsey, UK	CityFlyer Express (BA)	S	BMH
	Jersey European Airways	S	SVR
Hamburg, Germany	Deutsche BA (BA)	N	BA
Hanover, Germany	CityFlyer Express (BA)	S	BMH
Harare, Zimbabwe	Air Zimbabwe	S	GHI
	British Airways	N	BA
Havana, Cuba	Cubana/AOM	S	GHI
	British Airways	N	BA
Helsinki, Finland	Finnair	N	BA
Houston, USA	British Airways	N	BA
	Continental Airlines	S	SVR
Inverness, UK	British Airways	N	BA
Isle of Man	Jersey European Airways	S	SVR
Istanbul, Turkey	Azerbaijan Airlines	S	SVR
Jersey, UK	CityFlyer Express (BA)	S	BMH
	Jersey European Airways	S	SVR
Johannesburg, South Africa	African Star Airways	S	
Kathmandu, Nepal	Royal Nepal Airlines	N	BA
Kiev, Ukraine	British Airways	N	BA
	Ukraine International	S	SVR
Kingston, Jamaica	British Airways	N	BA
Krakow, Poland	LOT	N	BA
Kristiansand, Norway	Maersk Air	N	GHI
La Coruna, Spain	European Regional Airlines	S	SVR
Lagos, Nigeria	British Airways	N	BA
Larnaca, Cyprus	Air 2000	N	GHI
	Cyprus Airways	S	SVR
Las Vegas, USA	Virgin Atlantic	S	BMH
Libreville, Gabon	Air Gabon	S	GHI
Lilongwe, Malawi	British Airways	N	BA
Lisbon, Portugal	GB Airways	N	BA
Ljubljana, Slovenia	British Airways	N	BA
Luanda, Angola	British Airways	N	BA
Lusaka, Zambia	British Airways	N	BA
Luxembourg	CityFlyer Express (BA)	S	BMH
Madrid, Spain	British Airways	N	BA
	Iberia	S	SVR
	Spanair	S	SVR
Mahé Island, Seychelles	Air Seychelles	S	GHI
	British Airways	N	BA
Malaga, Spain	GB Airways (BA)	N	BA
Male, Maldives	Air Maldives	S	

City/Country	Airline	North or South Terminal	Handling agent*
Malta	Air Malta	S	SVR
	GB Airways (BA)	N	BA
Manchester, UK	Air 2000	N	GHI
	British Airways	N	BA
Marrakech, Morocco	GB Airways (BA)	N	BA
Marseilles, France	Air Liberté	N	BA
Mauritius	British Airways	N	BA
Miami, USA	British Airways	N	BA
	Virgin Atlantic	S	BMH
Milan, Italy	British Airways	N	BA
	Alitalia	S	SVR
Minneapolis/St Paul, USA	Northwest Airlines	S	GHI
Minsk, Belarus	Belavia Airlines	S	GHI
Montego Bay, Jamaica	British Airways	N	BA
Montpellier, France	British Airways	N	BA
Moscow, Russia	British Airways	N	BA
	Transaero Airlines	S	GHI
Munich, Germany	Deutsche BA (BA)	N	BA
Murcia, Spain	GB Airways (BA)	N	BA
Nairobi, Kenya	British Airways	N	BA
Nantes, Farnce	BritAir/Air France	N	GHI
	GB Airways (BA)	N	BA
Naples, Italy	British Airways	N	BA
Nassau, Bahamas	British Airways	N	BA
Newcastle upon Tyne, UK	CityFlyer Express (BA)	S	BMH
Newquay, UK	Brymon Airways (BA)	N	BA
New York/Newark, USA	British Airways	N	BA
	Continental Airlines	S	SVR
	Virgin Atlantic	S	BMH
Nice, France	British Airways	N	BA
Orlando, USA	British Airways	N	BA
	Virgin Atlantic	S	BMH
Oslo, Norway	British Airways	N	BA
Oviedo, Spain	Air Nostrum/Iberia	S	SVR
Palma de Mallorca, Spain	Air Europa	S	GHI
	GB Airways (BA)	N	BA
Paphos, Cyprus	Air 2000	N	GHI
	Cyprus Airways	S	SVR
Paris (Charles de Gaulle), France	British Airways	N	BA
	Cameroon Airlines	S	SVR
Philadelphia, USA	US Airways	S	GHI
Phoenix, USA	British Airways	N	BA
Pisa, Italy	British Airways	N	BA
Pittsburgh, USA	US Airways	S	GHI
Plymouth, UK	Brymon (BA)	N	BA
Porto, Portugal	GB Airways (BA)	N	BA

City/Country	Airline	North or South Terminal	Handling agent*
Raleigh/Durham, USA	American Airlines	S	SVR
Riga, Latvia	British Airways	N	BA
Rio de Janeiro, Brazil	British Airways	N	BA
Rome, Italy	British Airways	N	BA
	Deutsche BA	N	BA
Rotterdam, Netherlands	CityFlyer Express (BA)	S	BMH
St Louis, USA	TWA	S	GHI
St Lucia, Windward Islands	British Airways	N	BA
	Virgin Atlantic	S	BMH
St Petersburg, Russia	Aeroflot	S	GHI
	British Airways	N	BA
Salzburg, Austria	British Airways	N	BA
Sanaa, Republic of Yemen	Yemenia Airways	S	SVR
San Diego, USA	British Airways	N	BA
San José, Costa Rica	British Airways	N	BA
San Juan, Puerto Rico	British Airways	N	BA
Santiago, Chile	British Airways	N	BA
Sao Paulo, Brazil	British Airways	N	BA
Seville, Spain	GB Airways (BA)	N	BA
Shannon, Republic of Ireland	CityFlyer Express (BA)	S	BMH
Skopje, Macedonia	British Airways	N	BA
Sofia, Bulgaria	British Airways	N	BA
Stockholm, Sweden	British Airways	N	BA
Tallinn, Estonia	Estonian Air	S	GHI
Tampa, USA	British Airways	N	BA
Tangier, Morocco	GB Airways (BA)	N	BA
Tel Aviv, Israel	British Airways	N	BA
Tobago, Trinidad & Tobago	British Airways	N	BA
Toulouse, France	Air Liberté	N	BA
Trieste, Italy	British Airways	N	BA
Tripoli, Libyan Arab Jamahiriya	British Airways	N	BA
Tunis, Tunisia	GB Airways (BA)	N	BA
Turin, Italy	National Jets Italia	S	SVR
Valencia, Spain	GB Airways (BA)	N	BA
Venice, Italy	Alitalia	S	SVR
Verona, Italy	British Airways	N	BA
Vienna, Austria	British Airways	N	BA
	Lauda Air	S	SVR
Vilnius, Lithuania	British Airways	N	BA
Zagreb, Croatia	British Airways	N	BA
Zurich, Switzerland	British Airways	N	BA
	Air Seychelles	S	GHI

* Handling agent abbreviations: BA — British Airways
BMH — British Midland Handling Services
GHI — Gatwick Handling International
SVR — Servisair

Aircraft

Airbus A300B4-600 — (Monarch Airlines)

Airbus A310 — (Air Maldives, Cyprus Airways, Yemenia)

Airbus A319 and A320 — (Air 2000, Caledonian, Cyprus Airways, Airtours International Airways, Finnair, GB Airways, JMC Airlines [formerly Caledonian Airways and Flying Colours], Monarch Airlines, Virgin Sun)

Airbus A321 — (Air 2000, Finnair, GB Airways, Monarch Airlines)

Airbus A330-200 — (Emirates, Canada 3000 Airlines, Airtours International Airways, Monarch Airlines)

Airbus A330-300 — (US Airways — from May 2000)

ATR-42 — (Air France, CityFlyer Express)

ATR-72 — (CityFlyer Express)

Avro RJ100 (BAe146 Srs 300) — (CityFlyer Express, Jersey European Airways)

BAe146 Srs 100/200 — (Jersey European Airways, Flightline/Palmair)

BAe Jetstream 31 — (Base Airlines)

BAC One-Eleven 500 — (European Air Charter)

Boeing 727-200 — (Sabre Airways)

Boeing 737-200 — (Croatia Airlines, Ryanair, Transaero)

Boeing 737-300 — (Air Europa, Air Malta, British Airways, Deutsche BA, easyJet Airlines, GB Airways/BA, Lauda Air, Maersk Air, Transavia, Ukraine International Airlines)

Boeing 737-400 — (Air Europa, British Airways, Futura, GB Airways/BA, LOT Polish Airlines, Malev Hungarian Airlines)

Boeing 737-500 — (Aer Lingus, Estonian Air, LOT Polish Airlines, Maersk Air, Malev Hungarian Airlines)

Boeing 737-800 — (Ryanair, Transavia, Sabre Airways)

Boeing 747-200 — (Air Gabon, Cameroon Airlines, Garuda Indonesia, Virgin Atlantic, Air Atlanta Iceland, Tower Air)

Boeing 747-400 — (British Airways)

Boeing 757-200 and-300 — (Air 2000, Azerbaijan Airlines, Continental Airlines, Finnair, Royal Nepal Airlines, Air Transat, Canada 3000 Airlines, Royal Aviation, Britannia Airways, JMC Airlines [formerly Flying Colours], Monarch Airlines, American Trans Air)

Boeing 767-200 and -200ER — (Air Gabon, Air Zimbabwe, American Airlines, TWA, US Airways, Britannia Airways)

Boeing 767-300ER — (Air Seychelles, Air 2000, British Airways, Delta Air Lines, Canadian Airlines, Airtours International Airways, Britannia Airways)

Boeing 777 — (American Airlines, British Airways, Continental Airlines, Delta Air Lines)

Bombardier de Havilland Dash 8Q-300 — (Brymon Airways/BA)

Bombardier/Canadair RJ100/RJ200 — (Brit Air/Air France, Iberia/Air Nostrum, Lauda Air)

Embraer EMB120 Brasilia — (Base Airlines)

Embraer RJ145 — (European Regional Airlines)

Fokker F27 Friendship — (Channel Express)

Fokker 100 — (Air Liberté/BA)

BAe125 Srs 700 — (Interflight)

Ilyushin Il-62 — (Aeroflot)

Ilyushin Il-86 — (Aeroflot)

Lockheed L-1011 500 TriStar — (Air Transat, Air Atlanta Iceland, Royal Aviation, American Trans Air)

McDonnell Douglas DC-10-10 and -30 — (Continental Airlines, Cubana/AOM, Monarch, Northwest Airlines, JMC Airlines [formerly Caledonian Airways], Sun Country Airlines)

McDonnell Douglas MD-11 — (Delta Air Lines, World Airways

McDonnell Douglas MD-82/83 — (Alitalia, Finnair, Meridiana, Spanair)

Tupolev Tu-134 — (Aeroflot)

Tupolev Tu-154M — (Aeroflot, Azerbaijan Airlines, Belavia Belarussian Airlines)

Aircraft Type Specifications and Details for Aircraft regularly seen at Gatwick

Airbus A300B4-600

Manufacturer: Airbus Industrie

Engines: 2 x 61,500lb-thrust General Electric CF6-50C2 or 58,000lb Pratt & Whitney JT9D59A

No of passengers: 266 in typical two-class accommodation. 361 maximum

Wingspan: 44.84m

Length: 54.08m

Max take-off weight: 170,500kg

Empty weight: 90,300kg

Range with max payload: 6,171km

Number in service: 520 ordered/483 delivered (all Airbus A300/310 variants)

The original Airbus, launched in May 1969 as a 250-seater, first flew at Toulouse, France in October 1972. The first production variant, the A300B2, entered service with TEA of Belgium in May 1974. Many older A300s are now being converted to freighters. The A310 is a smaller, 210-seat development of the A300B4 that entered service with Swissair and Lufthansa in April 1983. The A300-600 first entered service in 1988.

Airbus A320 family (A319/A320/A321)

Manufacturer: Airbus Industrie

Engines: A319-100 — 2 x 23,480lb CFM56-5A5 or 5B6. 2 x 26,990lb CFM56-5B7. 2 x IAE V2524-A5

A320-200 — 2 x 26,490lb IAE V2527-A5. 2 x CFM56-5A3 or 5B4

A321-200 — 2 x 31,980lb CFM56-5B3. 2 x 32,990lb IAE V2533-A5

No of passengers: A319-100 — 124 in typical two-class accommodation. 145 maximum

A320-200 — 150 in typical two-class accommodation. 180 maximum

A321-200 — 185 in typical two-class accommodation. 220 maximum

Wingspan: A319/320/321 — 34.1m

Length: A319 — 33.84m
         A320 — 37.57m
         A321 — 44.51m

Max take-off weight: A319 — 75,500kg
                      A320 — 77,000kg
                      A321 — 89,000kg

Below: *Airbus A300-605R G-MONS (ex-VH-YMK), one of three operated by Monarch Airlines, July 1999. Geoffrey P. Jones*

Above: *Airbus A330-243 A6-EKR of Emirates climbs after take-off from Runway 08, November 1999. Geoffrey P. Jones*

Empty weight: A319 — 40,350kg
               A320 — 42,100kg
               A321 — 48,080kg

Range with max payload:
   A319 — 4,570km
   A320 — 3,990km
   A321 — 3,620km

Number in service:
   A319 — 603 ordered/145 delivered
   A320 — 1,220 ordered/743 delivered
   A321 — 264 ordered/136 delivered

The 150-seat A320 was launched in 1984 by a European consortium including France, Germany, UK and Spain, the world's first subsonic, fly-by-wire airliner and the first to use large amounts of composite material for primary structures. The prototype A320 first flew in February 1987 and entered service with Air France a year later. The stretched-fuselage A321 entered service with Lufthansa in March 1994. The smaller A319 was launched in June 1993 and entered service with Swissair in May 1996. An even smaller 100-seat version, the A318 was launched in April 1999 and has orders for over 157, including from BA which will introduce the type in 2003. Final assembly of these Airbuses is in France and Germany, the A320 at Toulouse (Aérospatiale) and A319/A321 at Hamburg (Dasa Airbus). Some A319 production will be moved from Hamburg to Toulouse when A318 production commences at Hamburg. Finnair introduced its A319s on services from Helsinki to Gatwick in late 1999.

Airbus A330 (330-200 and 330-300)

Manufacturer: Airbus Industrie

Engines: A330-200 — 2 x 67,980lb Pratt & Whitney PW4168A or 72,990lb PW4173.

2 x 69,890lb General Electric CF6-80E1. 2 x 71,000lb Rolls-Royce Trent 772

A330-300 — 2 x 68,090lb Pratt & Whitney PW4000. 2 x 71,010lb Rolls-Royce Trent 772

2 x 69,880lb General Electric CF6-80E1

No of passengers: A330-200 — 253/293 respectively in typical three/two-class accommodation. 380 maximum

Wingspan: 60.3m

Length: A330-200 — 59m
           A330-300 — 63.7m

Max take-off weight: 230,000kg

Empty weight: A330-200 — 120,500kg
                 A330-300 — 124,300kg

Range with max payload:
   A330-200 — 7,800km
   A330-300 — 6,850km

Number in service: A330-200/300 — 257 ordered/108 delivered

Launched at the same time as the four-engined Airbus A340 in June 1987, the first A330-300 was flown in November 1992, entering commercial service in January 1994 with Air France. The A330-200 is a slightly smaller, but longer-range version that was first flown in August 1997 and delivered initially to

Above: *ATR-72 G-BVTK of CityFlyer Express in British Airways Express colours, June 1999.* Geoffrey P. Jones

Canada 3000 in April 1998. Final assembly of the A330 takes place at Toulouse (Aérospatiale). US Airways will introduce A330-300s on Gatwick services in summer 2000.

Avions de Transport Regional ATR-42 and ATR-72

Manufacturer: Avions de Transport Regional

Engines: ATR-42-320 and 500 — 2 x 1602kW Pratt & Whitney Canada PW121 turboprop or PW127E

ATR-72-500 — 2 x 2049kW Pratt & Whitney Canada PW127 turboprop

No of passengers:
ATR-42 — 42. 50 maximum
ATR-72 — 68. 74 maximum

Wingspan: ATR-42 — 24.57m

Length: ATR-42 — 22.67m
ATR-72 — 27.05m
ATR-72 — 27.17m

Max take-off weight:
ATR-42-320 — 16,700kg
ATR-72 — 22,000kg

Empty weight: ATR-42-320 — 10,790kg
ATR-72 — 12,850kg

Range with max payload:
ATR-42-320 — 926km
ATR-72-500 — 1,683km

Number in service:
ATR-42 — 356 ordered/344 delivered
ATR-72 — 249 ordered/226 delivered

A consortium of Aérospatiale Matra from France and Alenia from Italy was formed in 1981, the prototype ATR-42 first flying in August 1984 and entering service in December 1985. The stretched version, the ATR-72, first flew in October 1988. The aircraft are assembled at Aérospatiale Matra in Toulouse. Xian Aircraft in China manufactures rear fuselages and may establish a final assembly line in China. BA's wholly owned subsidiary, CityFlyer Express, flies both the ATR-42 and ATR-72 from Gatwick.

British Aerospace BAe146/Avro RJ100

Manufacturer: British Aerospace Regional Aircraft

Engines: BAe146-100 — 4 x 6970lb Allied Signal ALF502 turbofan

Avro RJ100 — 4 x 7000lb Allied Signal LF5071F turbofan

No of passengers: BAe146-100 — 73 in typical two-class accommodation. 84 maximum

Avro RJ100 — 100 in typical two-class accommodation. 112 maximum

Wingspan: 26.34m

Length: BAe146-100 — 26.2m
Avro RJ100 — 31m

Max take-off weight:
BAe146-100 — 38,102kg
Avro RJ100 — 44,225kg

Empty weight:
BAe146-100 — 23,400kg
Avro RJ100 — 25,620kg

Range with max payload:
BAe146-100 — 1,450km
Avro RJ100 — 2,170km

Number in service:
BAe146 — 219 delivered/216 in service
RJ85/100 — 154 ordered/131 delivered

The BAe146-100 prototype first flew in September 1981 and first entered service with Dan-Air in May 1983. Production ceased in 1993 after 219 examples of the 100, 200 and 300 Series had been built. The Avro RJ family was developed from the BAe146, the first 70-passenger RJ70 flying in July 1992. Crossair took delivery of its first RJ85 in April 1993. The larger RJ100 can seat between 100 and 112 passengers. The main operators of these types at Gatwick are Jersey European Airways and BA wholly-owned subsidiary CityFlyer Express, both operating from the southern finger of the South Terminal.

Boeing 727-200

Manufacturer: Boeing Commercial Airplane Group

Engines: 3 x 16,180lb Pratt & Whitney JT8D17 turbofan

No of passengers: 145 in typical two-class accommodation. 189 maximum

Wingspan: 32.92m

Length: 46.69m

Max take-off weight: 76,655kg

Empty weight: 42,514kg

Range with max payload: 1,820km

Number in service: 1,831 delivered (all models)/1,378 in service

The tri-jet Boeing 727-100 prototype first flew in February 1963 and entered service the following year. Large numbers are still in service in the Americas and other parts of the world increasingly used in its converted form as a freighter but it is now infrequently seen in the UK partly due to more stringent engine noise regulations although some 727s have been retro-fitted with BF Goodrich Super 27 'silenced' engines. The only airline regularly using 727-200s at Gatwick is Sabre Airways.

Boeing 737-300/400/500 (Classic)

Manufacturer: Boeing Commercial Airplane Group

Engines: 737-300 — 2 x 22,000lb CFM International CFM56-3B1 or 23,370lb CFM56-3C1 turbofan

737-400 & 500 — 2 x 23,370lb CFM International CFM56-3C1 turbofan

No of passengers: 737-300 — 126 in typical two-class accommodation. 149 maximum

737-400 — 147 in typical two-class accommodation. 168 maximum

737-500 — 110 in typical two-class accommodation. 132 maximum

Wingspan: 737-300/400/500 — 28.88m

Length: 737-300 — 33.4m
737-400 — 36.45m
737-500 — 31.0m

Max take-off weight:
737-300 — 62,820kg
737-400 — 68,040kg
737-500 — 60,550kg

Empty weight: 737-300 — 49,710kg
737-400 — 34,810kg
737-500 — 31,950kg

Above: *D-ADBR is one of 21 Boeing 737-300s operated by Deutsche BA, November 1999.* Geoffrey P. Jones

Range with max payload:
  737-300 — 4,184km
  737-400 — 3,846km
  737-500 — 4,450km

Number in service: 737-300 — 1,118
  737-400 — 484
  737-500 — 386

The prototype Boeing 737-100 first flew in April 1967. After 30 examples were built production switched to the larger 737-200, powered by two Pratt & Whitney JT8Ds, this model remaining in production until 1988. It was superseded by the CFM56-powered 737-300, the first flight of which was in February 1984, with first deliveries to USAir. The first flight of the 737-400 was in September 1988, with first deliveries to Piedmont Airlines (which became part of USAir). British Airways' entire 34-strong fleet of 737-400s is now based at Gatwick. The first flight of the shorter-fuselage 737-500 was in June 1989 with first deliveries to Southwest Airlines in the USA. Maersk Air was one of the first European customers for the 737-500. Production of these three Classic 737 models has been at Boeing's Renton plant near Seattle but was completed at the end of 1999 with a total of 1,988 examples being built.

**Boeing 737NG (600/700/800)
(Next Generation)**
Manufacturer: Boeing Commercial Airplane Group

Engines: 737-600 — 2 x 19,480lb CFM International CFM56-7B18 or 20,580lb CFM56-7B20 turbofan

737-700 — 2 x 20,590lb CFM International CFM56-7B20 or 24,180lb CFM56-7B24 turbofan

737-800 — 2 x 24,180lb CFM International CFM56-7B24 or 26,290lb CFM56-7B26 turbofan

No of passengers: 737-600 — 110 in typical two-class accommodation. 132 maximum

737-700 — 126 in typical two-class accommodation. 149 maximum

737-800 — 162 in typical two-class accommodation. 189 maximum

Wingspan: 737-600/700/800 — 34.31m

Length: 737-600 — 31.2m
  737-700 — 33.6m
  737-800 — 39.5m

Max take-off weight:
  737-600 — 56,240kg
  737-700 — 60,320kg
  737-800 — 70,530kg

Empty weight: 737-600 — 37,100kg
  737-700 — 38,150kg
  737-800 — 41,150kg

Range with max payload:
  737-600 — up to 5,917km
  737-700 — up to 5,926km
  737-800 — up to 5,370km

Number ordered: 737-600 — 116
  737-700 — 393
  737-800 — 373

Superseding the 737 Classics (737-300/400/500), the programme was launched in November 1993 with the first 737NG (Next Generation), a 737-700, flying for the first time in February 1997

Left: *Although North American Airlines Boeing 737-800s do not fly to Gatwick, this example of the 737NG (N800NA) illustrates the fuselage stretch when compared with the 737 Classic.*
Geoffrey P. Jones

Above: Virgin's first aircraft, G-VIRG, Boeing 747-287B Maiden Voyager, November 1999. Geoffrey P. Jones

and being delivered to launch-customer Southwest Airlines in December 1997. Boeing 737NGs feature a new enlarged wing, new engines, higher cruising speeds and greater range capabilities. The 737-600 was known as the 737-500X initially — launch customer for the 737-600 was SAS, which took delivery of its first aircraft in September 1998. The 737-800 was first flown in July 1997 and the first was delivered in April 1998 to Hapag-Lloyd in Germany. The ultimate 737NG is the 737-900, with seating for up to 189 passengers (but normally 177) and which is due to enter airline service in April 2001 with Alaska Airlines. A business-jet version of the 737 is also flying, the Boeing BBJ, and several production 737s have been sold as corporate transports. By late 1999 over 1,200 737NGs had been ordered and 350 delivered.

Boeing 747-200 Classic

Manufacturer: Boeing Commercial Airplane Group

Engines: 4 x 55.060lb Pratt & Whitney JT9D-7 or 4 x 50,110lb Rolls-Royce RB211-524 or 4 x 52,360lb General Electric CF6-50E turbofan

No of passengers: 374 in typical three-class accommodation. 490 maximum

Wingspan: 59.64m

Length: 70.7m

Max take-off weight: 351,535kg

Empty weight: 171,460kg

Range with max payload: 11,000km

Number in service:
747-100/SP/200/300 — 724 delivered/603 in service

The original Jumbo Jet, the prototype Boeing 747-100 first flew in February 1969 with P&W JT9 engines and the first of an order for 25 entered service with Pan Am in January 1970 with a flightdeck crew of three including a flight engineer. The 747-200 was a subsequent heavier and longer-range version which entered service in January 1971 and was available with a choice of engines, including Rolls-Royce RB211s. Some versions of the 747-200 were mixed passenger/freight variants (Combis) and others, including those of Northwest Airlines, were dedicated 100% freighters. A short-fuselage, long-range version was the 747SP. The last 747 Classic was manufactured by Boeing in 1991. Many of the airlines to first establish transatlantic scheduled services to Gatwick flew 747 Classics including Continental, Northwest and PEOPLExpress. Virgin Atlantic and BA are now the main users of the type at Gatwick.

Boeing 747-400

Manufacturer: Boeing Commercial Airplane Group

Engines: 4 x 57,080lb Pratt & Whitney PW4056 or 63,150lb PW4062 or 4 x 59,320lb Rolls-Royce RB211-524H/T or 56,180lb RB211-524G/T or 4 x 57,080lb General Electric CF6-80C2 turbofan

Above: *Boeing 747-436 G-BNLJ of British Airways.* Geoffrey P. Jones

No of passengers: 416 in typical three-class accommodation

Wingspan: 64.4m

Length: 70.7m

Max take-off weight: 396,900kg

Empty weight: 181,120kg

Range with max payload: 10,460km

Number in service:
567 ordered/491 delivered

Developed from the 747-300 but with completely redesigned two-crew glass cockpit, extensive use of composites in construction, a resultant reduction in empty weight and many aerodynamic enhancements, including a 4.9m increase in wingspan from the 'Classic' and the easily identifiable wing-tip winglets. The 747-400 is assembled at Boeing's Everett plant in Washington State, the first example was flown in April 1988 and the first delivered to launch customer Northwest Airlines in January 1989. A further stretch of the 747-400 is currently under consideration by Boeing, the 747-400X, seating 70 more passengers, and having a range of up to 14,800km and an increased gross weight. The only regular operator of the type at Gatwick is BA. Although Virgin Atlantic has six 747-400s in its fleet, these are usually based at Heathrow.

Boeing 757-200/-300

Manufacturer: Boeing Commercial Airplane Group
Engines: 2 x 43,480lb Rolls-Royce RB211-535E4B or 2 x 40,090lb Pratt & Whitney PW2040 turbofan

No of passengers: 201 in typical two-class accommodation. 231 maximum

Wingspan: 38.0m

Length: 47.3m

Max take-off weight: 115,660kg

Empty weight: 58,390kg

Range with max payload: 7,050km

Number in service:
967 ordered/872 delivered

A development of and successor to the tri-jet Boeing 727, the launch customers for the 757 were Eastern Air Lines and BA. The prototype first flew in February 1982 and the type entered service first with Eastern in January 1983. As loads grew it became increasingly popular with many of the holiday and IT charter airlines, superseding their Boeing 737s in the case of both Britannia and Monarch. BA's fleet of 757s is now being replaced and it no longer operates them from Gatwick. Boeing assembles 757s at Renton, near Seattle and has developed a stretched-fuselage (7.1m longer) version, the 757-300, which was first introduced in service by German airline Condor Flugdienst in March 1999. JMC Airlines have also ordered the 757-300. Many 757s are used as freighters by operators such as DHL, Challenge Air Cargo, etc. The 757-200 can be seen operating with many airlines at Gatwick, including Air 2000, JMC Airlines, Air Transat and Monarch.

Boeing 767-200/300

Manufacturer: Boeing Commercial
Airplane Group

Engines: 767-200ER — 2 x 57,080lb Pratt
& Whitney PW4056 or 2 x 63,150lb
PW4062 or

2 x 62,020lb General Electric CF6-80C
turbofan

767-300ER — 2 x 57,080lb Pratt &
Whitney PW4056 or 63,150lb PW4062

or 2 x 62,020lb General Electric GCF6-
80C or

2 x 59,550lb Rolls-Royce RB211-
524G/H turbofan

No of passengers: 767-200ER — 181 in
typical three-class accommodation.
255 maximum

767-300ER — 218 in typical three-
class accommodation. 350 maximum

Wingspan: 47.57m

Length: 767-200ER — 48.51m
767-300ER — 54.94m

Max take-off weight:
767-200ER — 179,170kg

Empty weight: 767-200ER — 84,690kg
767-300ER — 186,880kg
767-300ER — 90,540kg

Range with max payload:
767-200ER — 12,328km
767-300ER — 10,992km

Number in service:
872 ordered/754 delivered

The standard P&W JT9D and
GE CF6-powered early
versions of the Boeing 767
first flew in September 1981
and entered service with
United Airlines in 200/220-
seat configurations in August
1982. Manufacture takes
place at Boeing's Everett,
Washington plant. The first long-range
767-200ER entered service with Ethiopian
Airlines in May 1984. Britannia Airways
was one of the first to operate the 767
from Gatwick. The use of the 767-200ER
on transatlantic services to and from
Gatwick became popular, one of the first
services starting in June 1987 with
Piedmont Airlines. American Airlines and
TWA followed, as well as Delta Air Lines
more recently. Latest variant is the
767-400ER, involving a 6.4m stretch of
the fuselage from the 767-300ER. The
prototype was rolled out in August 1999
and first flew a couple of months later.
Delta Air Lines will take delivery of the
first aircraft in spring 2000.

Boeing 777-200

Manufacturer: Boeing Commercial
Airplane Group

Engines: 2 x 89,890lb Rolls-Royce Trent
892 or 2 x 93,800lb General Electric
GE90-94B or

2 x 90,110lb Pratt & Whitney PW4090
or 2 x 97,980lb PW4098 turbofan

No of passengers: 305 in typical three-
class accommodation. 440 maximum

Wingspan: 60.9m

Length: 63.73m

Max take-off weight: 297,560kg

Empty weight: 143,790kg

Above: *American Airlines first flew Boeing
777-223ERs to Gatwick in Summer 1999;
N771AN is pictured in July.*
Geoffrey P. Jones

Range with max payload:
11,040-13,237km

Number in service:
429 ordered/223 delivered

The world's largest twin-jet airliner is built at Boeing's Everett plant, Washington and first flew in June 1994. The first 777-200 was delivered to launch customer United Airlines in June 1995. British Airways put its first 777-200ER into service in February 1997 and 10 of the 777 fleet (currently numbering 25 and with a further 20 on order) are based at Gatwick for long-haul operations. Another 777 customer, Delta Air Lines, uses its aircraft on direct services from Gatwick to both Atlanta and Cincinnati, and American Airlines also started using 777s on Gatwick services during 1999. A stretched version, the 777-300, was launched by Boeing in June 1995, targeted at the Boeing 747 Classic replacement market — first deliveries to launch customer Cathay Pacific were in May 1998.

Bombardier/De Havilland Dash 8Q (DHC-8 Dash 8-300)

Manufacturer: Bombardier (De Havilland), Downsview, Ontario, Canada

Engines: 2 x 1,773kW Pratt & Whitney Canada PW123 or 2 x 1,864kW PW121 turboprop

No of passengers: 50 in typical two-class accommodation. 56 maximum

Wingspan: 27.43m

Length: 25.68m

Max take-off weight: 18,643kg

Empty weight: 11,709kg

Range with max payload: 1,483km

Number in service:
615 ordered/522 delivered

Originally the Dash 8 family, the first DHC-8-100 flew in June 1983 and entered service in October 1984. The DHC-8-200 was introduced in 1992 and the 50/60-seat DHC-8-300, with a 3.35m fuselage stretch in 1989, following its first flight in May 1987. Since 1998 Bombardier, now the parent of the former De Havilland Canada company, has designated the type as the Dash 8Q Series. A 70-seat Dash 8Q-400A was launched in 1995 and the prototype first flew in January 1998 with first deliveries to Uni Air and SAS Commuter in the autumn of 1999. Wholly owned BA subsidiary, Brymon Airways, flies its Dash 8Q-300s from Gatwick on services to Plymouth, Bristol and Newquay in South West England following the transfer of these services from Heathrow.

Bombardier/Canadair CRJ100/200 and CRJ700

Manufacturer: Bombardier (Canadair), Montreal, Quebec, Canada

Engines: CRJ100/200 — 2 x 9,210lb General Electric CF343 or 2 x 8,730lb GE CF343B1 turbofan

CRJ700 — 2 x 12,670lb General Electric CF348C1 turbofan

No of passengers: CRJ100/200 — 50-52
CRJ700 — 70-78

Left: Dash 8Q-311A G-BRYW of wholly owned BA subsidiary, Brymon Airways in June 1998.
Geoffrey P. Jones

Right: *Embraer ERJ145 Regional Jet G-EMBA, seen here at Southampton in January 2000, is the type operated into Gatwick by European Regional Airlines. This example it is in British Airways colours.*
Geoffrey P. Jones

Wingspan: CRJ100/200 — 21.21m

Length: CRJ100/200 — 26.77m
CRJ700 — 23.24m
CRJ700 — 32.51m

Max take-off weight: CRJ200 — 23,133kg

Empty weight: CRJ200 — 13,740kg
CRJ700 — 32,999kg
CRJ700 — 19,731kg

Range with max payload:
CRJ200 — 1,825km
CRJ700 — 3,154km

Number in service: CRJ all variants —
647 ordered/317 delivered

Developed from the Canadair Challenger business jet, the prototype, 50-seat CRJ100 first flew in May 1991 and was first delivered to Lufthansa Cityline in October 1992. A stretched, 70-seat version, the CRJ700 first flew at Montreal in May 1999 and is expected to enter service with launch customers BritAir (Air France) and American Eagle (American Airlines) in early 2001. CRJ100/200 operators at Gatwick include Iberia/Air Nostrum, BritAir (Air France) and Lauda Air.

Embraer ERJ135 and ERJ145

Manufacturer: Embraer, Sao José dos Campos, Brazil

Engines: 2 x 6,970lb Allison AE3007A turbofan

No of passengers: 50

Wingspan: 20.04m

Length: 29.87m

Max take-off weight: 19,200kg

Empty weight: 11,690kg

Range with max payload: 1,480km

Number in service:
293 ordered/132 delivered

Launched in June 1989 using the basic, but stretched fuselage (accommodating 49 seats) of the turboprop Embraer EMB120 Brasilia (30 seats), revised tail and new super-critical wing. The prototype ERJ145 first flew in August 1995 with first deliveries in early 1997 to Continental Express in the US. The smaller, 37-seat ERJ135 first flew in July 1998 with first deliveries, also to Continental Express, in July 1999. To date, 139 ERJ135s have been ordered and 10 delivered. ERJ145s have been sold extensively to European customers, including Regional Airlines of France, Sweden's Skyways, British Regional Airlines, Portugalia Airlines, Luxair and the Spanish regional airline European Regional Airlines based in Palma which operates services to Gatwick.

Fokker 100

Manufacturer: Fokker Aircraft, Schiphol, Netherlands. Declared bankrupt in March 1996.

Engines: 2 x 15,100lb Rolls-Royce Tay 650 turbofan

No of passengers: 109

Wingspan: 28.08m
Length: 35.53m

Max take-off weight: 44,450kg
Empty weight: 24,727kg

Range with max payload: 2,871km

Number in service:
277 delivered/274 in service

A development of the Fokker F28 Fellowship which first flew in November 1986 and was delivered to launch customers Swissair and USAir in 1988. Developments of the basic Fokker 100 included a version re-engined with the more powerful Tay 650 engine, and the 79-seat Fokker 70. This was first flown in April 1993, 47 having been built and delivered before production ceased. French airline, Air Liberté, in which BA has a majority shareholding, and which assimilated the routes and aircraft of TAT under a March 1998 merger, is the only scheduled operator of the Fokker 100 at Gatwick.

Ilyushin Il-62M (NATO name 'Classic')

Manufacturer: Ilyushin Design Bureau, Moscow

Engines: 4 x 23,370lb Aviadvigatel D-30KU turbofan

No of passengers: 114 in typical two-class accommodation. 195 maximum

Wingspan: 43.2m

Length: 53.12m

Max take-off weight: 167,000kg

Below: *Ilyushin Il62 CCCP-86501 is no longer current in the fleet of Aeroflot Russian International Airlines. Russian Il-62s are now registered in the RA- sequence.* Geoffrey P. Jones

Empty weight: 69,600kg

Range with max payload: 7,800km

Number in service: 285 delivered

A Russian clone of the British Vickers VC10 which was built between 1963 and 1985. Now largely obsolete but still operated by Aeroflot Russian International Airlines and several of the independent airlines of the Russian Federation.

Ilyushin Il-76T (NATO name 'Candid')

Manufacturer: Ilyushin Design Bureau, Moscow. Assembled by the Tashkent Aircraft Production Association (TAPO) in Tashkent, Uzbekistan.

Engines:
4 x 26,450lb Soloviev D-30KP turbofan

No of passengers: N/A freighter

Wingspan: 50.5m

Length: 46.59m

Max take-off weight: 170,000kg

Empty weight: 89,000kg

Range with max payload: 3,800km

Number in service: 285 delivered

Conceived as a military transport and first flown in March 1971. Commercial operations with Aeroflot began in December 1976. A 6.6m stretched version, the Il-76MF, was developed and first flown in August 1995. Occasionally seen at Gatwick on freight flights with a variety of eastern European airlines and those of the former Soviet Union.

Lockheed L-1011 500 TriStar

Manufacturer: Lockheed Martin, Marietta, Georgia, USA

Engines: 3 x 50,000lb Rolls-Royce RB211-524B4 turbofan

No of passengers: 256 in typical two-class accommodation. 330 maximum

Wingspan: 50.09m

Length: 50.057m

Max take-off weight: 231,330kg

Empty weight: 111,312kg

Range with max payload: 8,480km

Number in service: 249 delivered/189 in service

First flew in November 1970, one of the three classic wide-body jets of the time (the Boeing 747 and Douglas DC-10 were the others). Built between 1972 and 1983. The L-1011-500 is the extended-range version most frequently seen at Gatwick. Delta Air Lines used its L-1011s on services between Atlanta and Gatwick from April 1978 until superseded by McDonnell Douglas MD-11s in 1997 and more recently by Boeing 767-300s and 777s. Caledonian Airways, a TriStar operator at Gatwick, retired its last aircraft in 1999. Operators of the type at Gatwick, mainly on charter work, are the Canadian airlines Air Transat and Royal Aviation, as well as Air Atlanta Iceland and American Trans Air. The L-1011's days as a passenger airliner are numbered because of major airworthiness directives posted during 1999. A large number of former passenger L-1011s have now been converted to freighters, such as those flown by US airline Kitty Hawk International (formerly American International Airways — Kalitta).

McDonnell Douglas DC-8-71

Manufacturer: McDonnell Douglas, Long Beach, California (now Boeing)

Engines: 4 x 22,020lb CFM International CFM56-2C turbofan

No of passengers: 269. Freight payload 72,400kg

Wingspan: 43.4m

Length: 45.87m

Max take-off weight: 147,400kg

Empty weight: 75,000kg

Range with max payload: 6,296km

Number in service: 556 delivered/274 in service

The prototype Douglas DC-8 first flew in May 1958. Very few DC-8s are now left in passenger service. MK Air Cargo flies DC-8-50s, occasionally seen in the freight area at Gatwick. Because of noise limitations, many of the DC-8-61, DC-8-62 and DC-8-63s currently operational are the Commacorp CFM56 re-engined versions, respectively the DC-8-71, DC-8-72 and DC-8-73.

McDonnell Douglas DC-10-10/30 and Boeing MD-10

Manufacturer: McDonnell Douglas/Boeing, Long Beach, California

Engines:

DC-10-10 — 3 x 40,000lb General Electric CF6-6D turbofan

DC-10-30 — 3 x 51,010lb General Electric CF6-50C turbofan

DC-10-40 — 3 x 45,700lb or 47,200lb P&W JT9D-2059A turbofan

No of passengers: 250 in typical two-class accommodation. 380 maximum

Wingspan: DC-10-10 — 47.34m

Length: DC-10-10 — 55.5m
DC-10-30 — 50.4m
DC-10-30 — 55.3m

Max take-off weight:
DC-10-10 — 190,504kg

Empty weight: DC-10-10 — 111,344kg
DC-10-30 — 259,459kg
DC-10-30 — 121,563kg

Range with max payload:
DC-10-10 — 6,114km
DC-10-30 — 9,429km

Number in service: 446 delivered/410 in service (includes KC-10 military tankers)

The Douglas DC-10-10 tri-jet, wide-body, first flew in August 1970, was intended for short- and medium-range, high-density routes and first entered service with American Airlines in August 1971. Longer-range versions, the DC-10-30 and -40 were introduced in 1972 by Swissair and Northwest Airlines. Sixty KC-10 tanker versions were delivered to the USAF. Northwest Airlines and Continental Airlines have been regular users of the DC-10 on their services to Gatwick for many years. Continental DC-10-30s are maintained at Gatwick by FLS Aerospace (see Aircraft Maintenance). A major programme on older passenger DC-10-10s is underway to convert them to MD-10 freighters for freight/small package carrier FedEx.

McDonnell Douglas/Boeing MD-11

Manufacturer: Boeing — Douglas Products Division, Long Beach, California

Engines: 3 x 61,350lb General Electric CF6-80C2 or 3 x 60,000lb Pratt & Whitney PW4460 or

3 x 61,800lb PW4462 turbofan

No of passengers: 285 in typical three-class accommodation. 410 maximum

Wingspan: 51.7m

Length: 61.6m

Max take-off weight: 285,990kg

Empty weight: 132,800kg

Range with max payload:
11,100 to 13,160km

Number in service:
200 ordered/195 delivered

A stretched development of the Douglas DC-10, also with a two-crew flightdeck, first flown in January 1990 and first delivered to Finnair in December 1990.

Left: *In Delta Air Lines' former colour scheme, MD-11 N811DE nosed in at Gatwick's North Terminal, March 1998. Note the wingtip winglets which distinguish the MD-11 from the DC-10.* Geoffrey P. Jones

Right: *Three tail-mounted engines are a distinguishing feature of the Tupolev Tu-154; this is RA-85542 of Aeroflot.* Geoffrey P. Jones

Competition from the Airbus A340 and the Boeing 777 affected the aircraft's sales potential. Production is scheduled to end in early 2000 as orders have dried up and as part of Boeing's rationalisation, following its take-over of McDonnell Douglas in 1997. Delta Air Lines has a fleet of 15 MD-11s and these are regularly seen at Gatwick.

McDonnell Douglas/Boeing MD-80 series

Manufacturer: Boeing — Douglas Products Division, Long Beach, California

Engines: MD-82 — 2 x 20,900lb Pratt & Whitney JT8D-217A/C turbofan

MD-87 — 2 x 20,830lb JT8D-217B/C or 2 x 21,710lb Pratt & Whitney JT8D-219 turbofan

No of passengers: MD-82 — 144 in typical two-class accommodation. 172 maximum

MD-87 — 114 in typical two-class accommodation. 139 maximum

Wingspan: 32.8m

Length   MD-82 — 45.1m
MD-87 — 39.7m

Max take-off weight: MD-82 — 67,813kg

Empty weight: MD-82 — 37,925kg
MD-87 — 63,503kg
MD-87 — 35,313kg

Range with max payload:
MD-82 — 3,798km
MD-87 — 4,395km

Number in service: 1,191 delivered (excludes DC-9s and 134 MD-90s)

Developed progressively from the Douglas DC-9 which first flew in February 1965. The DC-9 Super 80 could carry up to 155 passengers and was renamed the DC-9-81 and then the McDonnell Douglas MD-81, entering service with Swissair in 1980. The MD-82 first entered service in August 1981 and then the shorter-fuselage MD-87 in late 1987. The MD-82 has been manufactured in greater numbers than any of the other variants, with 562 being built. Production of all these variants has now ceased and the MD-90 is expected to end production soon as Boeing concentrates on its MD-95 derivative, the Boeing 717-200. The main operators of MD-80s seen at Gatwick are Alitalia and Spanair.

Tupolev Tu-154M (NATO name 'Careless')

Manufacturer: Tupolev Joint Stock Co, Moscow. No longer in production.

Engines: 3 x 23,370lb Aviadvigatel D-30KU154-11 turbofan

No of passengers: 169 in typical two-class accommodation. 180 maximum

Wingspan: 37.5m

Length: 47.9m

Max take-off weight: 100,000kg

Empty weight: 55,300kg

Range with max payload: 3,740km

Number in service: 1,000+ delivered to both civil and military customers

First flown in October 1968 and powered by Kuznetsov NK-8 engines. An improved version, the Tu-154M, with Aviadvigatel D-30KU turbofans was first delivered to Aeroflot in 1984. An all-cargo version is the Tu-154S. Operated by Aeroflot and many of the independent airlines from the former Soviet Union. A few remain with CSA Czech Airlines and Malev, although the type is now rarely seen at Gatwick other than in Aeroflot colours.

Business Jets

While the use of Gatwick by private and corporate aircraft such as business or executive jets is diminishing, largely due to slot constraints and other commercial pressures on the airport, corporate aircraft activity can still be seen. These aircraft are usually parked at remote stands at the western extremity of the main apron or in the southern parts of the cargo ramp. Two main types of business or executive jet are most frequently seen at Gatwick as follows:

Gulfstream IV series

Manufacturer: Gulfstream Aerospace Corporation, Savannah, Georgia, USA

Engines: 2 x 13,850lb Rolls-Royce Tay Mk 611-8 turbofans

No of passengers: typically 13 business passengers. 19 maximum

Wingspan: 23.72m

Length: 26.92m

Max take-off weight: 33,838kg

Empty weight: 16,100kg

Range with max payload: 7,815km (3 crew + 8 passengers)

Number in service: 750+ all models

The Grumman G-1159 Gulfstream II intercontinental business jet first flew in October 1966 with two Rolls-Royce Spey turbofans. The Gulfstream III, with a 24in

(610mm) fuselage stretch and NASA winglets first flew in December 1979. Several company ownership changes have taken place since Grumman flew the Gulfstream II prototype. One of the current production models, the Gulfstream IV is a basic Gulfstream II fuselage with a 54in (1,372mm) stretch, an extra cabin window on each side and RR Tay engines. Nearly 300 of this model have been sold. The latest development is the long-range (12,038km) Gulfstream V, first flown in November 1995 and of which approximately 35 have now been delivered.

Raytheon Hawker 800

Manufacturer: Raytheon Aircraft Co, Wichita, Kansas, USA

Engines: 2 x 4,660lb Allied Signal TFE731-5BR turbofans

No of passengers: mid-size business jet for 4 or 6 passengers. Max 10

Wingspan: 15.65m

Length: 15.6m

Max take-off weight: 12,700kg

Empty weight: 7,323kg

Range with max payload: 4,639km

Number in service: 1,050+ of all models

Starting life as the DH125 executive jet and first flying in August 1962, the design was taken over and progressively developed by Hawker Siddeley and then British Aerospace, although the aircraft was still generically known as the 125. Its last models were the BAe125 Srs 800 and BAe1000. In August 1993 British Aerospace sold its 125 assets and design rights to Raytheon Aircraft (formerly Beech Aircraft Corporation). Production was transferred from the UK to Wichita, USA in 1995 and the first model built there is known as the Hawker 800XP, basically a BAe125 Srs 800. The 1,000th 125 business jet was delivered by Raytheon in 1998.

Airlines

British Airways

British Airways (BA), its subsidiaries and franchise partners now operate around 47% of the take-off and landing slots at Gatwick Airport. The airline's current dominance at Gatwick has grown steadily from small beginnings in the 1950s, almost mirroring the growth of the airport itself. BA is also dominant at Gatwick's North Terminal. Currently, around 70 BA aircraft are based at Gatwick: 19 Boeing 747-400s, 10 Boeing 777s, four Boeing 767s, and 37 assorted models of Boeing 737. BA's short-/medium-haul operations at Gatwick are unofficially known as Euro-Gatwick, created from Dan-Air, and kept separate from mainline BA (see History).

In 1935, several smaller UK-based airlines merged to form the first British Airways and became Imperial Airways' principal competitor on European routes, operating from Gatwick rather than from London's other airports at the time, Croydon and Heston (see History). Today's British Airways was created in 1972 when British Overseas Airways

Corporation (BOAC) and British European Airways (BEA) were combined. Immediately prior to this, in 1967, the government had recommended a holding board be established to become responsible for these two main British airlines. It also recommended the establishment of a second-force airline, to be brought about by the unification of various independent airlines. As a result, British Caledonian was founded in 1970, based at Gatwick, when the original Caledonian Airways took over British United Airways (BUA). In July 1979, the government announced its intention to sell shares in BA and the Civil Aviation Act 1980 was passed to enable this to happen.

As a result of the 1946 Civil Aviation Bill, BEA had been created as a public corporation. Early BEA operations from

Below: *BA activity at the North Terminal in March 1998, with a Boeing 747 Classic in the airline's former livery nosed in.* Geoffrey P. Jones

Gatwick are detailed in the History section but the other state-owned airline, BOAC, did not use Gatwick at all in the 1960s and 1970s, apart from the occasional bad-weather diversion from Heathrow.

The only other BEA services from Gatwick included a short-lived service to Cologne/Bonn and onwards to Hanover in the summer of 1959, a service to Paris in the summer of 1961 and a service to Dinard (France) between May 1959 and October 1963.

As the charter airlines and other scheduled airlines such as Dan-Air and BUA started to establish strong footholds at Gatwick, BEA's presence was largely limited to its services to the Channel Islands. Its services to Jersey and Guernsey were being flown from both Gatwick and Heathrow and by 1971 Channel Islands flights numbered 82 per week from the two London airports.

Following the formation of BA, it was privatised in February 1987 and in the same year, merged with British Caledonian. With the strong British Caledonian presence at Gatwick now under the BA banner and with the rapid growth of British Airtours, a huge BA presence at Gatwick was quickly established.

Above: *About to land on Runway 26 at Gatwick, BA Boeing 737-436 G-DOCH with its 'Grand Union' tail design.* Geoffrey P. Jones

BEA Airtours was formed as a subsidiary of BEA in April 1969 and flew DH106 Comet 4 inclusive tour (IT) charter flights almost exclusively from Gatwick to traditional Mediterranean and Canary Island destinations. In December 1971, the first former BOAC Boeing 707 arrived at Gatwick to join the BEA Airtours fleet. The last season that the Comets flew with BEA Airtours was 1973 and then seven Boeing 707s were used to operate the IT flights to southern Europe, the Canaries and North Africa. With the formation of BA in 1974, this limb of the company changed its name from BEA Airtours to British Airtours and by the early 1980s Boeing 737-200s and L-1011 TriStars were flying from Gatwick in this livery.

The opening of Gatwick's new North Terminal by HM the Queen in 1988 was a watershed year for both BA and Gatwick. BA moved almost wholesale to the North Terminal, British Airtours operation was assimilated into Caledonian Airways and

Above: *Taxying in towards its parking stand at the North Terminal is BA Boeing 747-400 G-CIVU. The wingtip winglets and stretched upper deck are two of the immediately noticeable features that distinguish this version of the 747 from the older 747-200 series, or 747 Classic as it is now known. Geoffrey P. Jones*

Above: *BA has 10 of its Boeing 777 fleet based at Gatwick for medium-/long-haul services. G-VIIA, a 777-236IGW (increased gross weight), is seen here in April 1999 in front of the southern arm of the North Terminal. Geoffrey P. Jones*

the Airtours name disappeared. BA then transferred all services from Gatwick to Jeddah, Riyadh and Tokyo to Heathrow, and the Islamabad, Bermuda, Nassau, Cairo, Luxor, Amman, Khartoum, Larnaca and Athens services from Heathrow to Gatwick. Former British Caledonian short-haul services from Gatwick were transferred by the Civil Aviation Authority to other airlines.

Increasing competition from BA at Gatwick is popularly ascribed as one of the reasons for the November 1992 failure of Dan-Air. BA stepped in to the void left

by this airline, acquired some of its Gatwick-based aircraft, the routes and some of the staff. The March 1991 failure of Air Europe, which had developed scheduled services from Gatwick, as well as charter flights, was another event that immediately benefited BA's expansion at Gatwick in the early 1990s.

During the 1990s, BA strengthened its position and its breadth of services from Gatwick. In May 1992, BA took a 49% stake in the former German airline, Delta Air Regionalflugverkehr and renamed it Deutsche BA and since April 1998, BA has owned 100% of the company. Also in 1992, BA acquired a 49% holding in the leading French independent airline TAT European, a holding subsequently increased to 100%. BA formed an alliance with USAir in 1993 and took over that airline's former Piedmont service from Gatwick to Charlotte (North Carolina, USA). In February 1995, GB Airways became a BA franchisee with their services from Gatwick to Spain and North Africa developed further. French airline, Air Liberté, filed for bankruptcy in September 1996, but BA stepped in and acquired a majority stake in it the following month. A merger of TAT European and Air Liberté under the latter's name was completed in March 1998. BA agreed to sell Air Liberté to Taitbout Antibes in May 2000.

Plymouth-based Brymon Airways merged with Birmingham European Airways in 1992 and commenced trading under the Brymon European Airways name but the merger was dissolved in 1993 when Brymon became a wholly owned subsidiary of BA. Two of its core services had been from London Heathrow to Plymouth and Newquay. As part of its plan to free up valuable landing slots at Heathrow, BA moved Brymon's DHC-8 services to the South West from Heathrow to Gatwick. The most recent of BA's acquisitions has been its former franchised operator, CityFlyer Express (see separate section following). On 28 October 1999, the Secretary of State for Trade and Industry approved BA's purchase of CityFlyer Express for £75 million, following BA's initial take-over proposal a year earlier.

During the years 1995 to 1999, BA's operation at Gatwick, measured by the number of seats available, increased by 130%. The total number of passengers had increased by more than 75%, and now with its six partner airlines, BA's group operations at Gatwick span 127

Above: *Looking east along this line of tails of Boeing 737s, 767s and 777s, the BA-dominated North Terminal is a colourful spectacle with BA's World Image artwork. These eventually totalled a portfolio of over 50 different designs following the launch of this new image on 10 June 1997. In 1999, following considerable adverse publicity about these designs, BA decided to standardise on the Union Flag tail design as first applied to its Concorde aircraft. The second and fifth tails from the left (a 737-400 and a 777) feature this design.* BA

Above: *British Airways Business and First Class passengers can utilize the airline's recently opened Terraces lounge at the North Terminal prior to their flights; this is the reception area. Many of the other major scheduled airlines using Gatwick have their own lounges for the use of Business Class passengers.* BA

Right: *BA's Terraces lounge at the North Terminal where Business and First Class passengers can relax prior to a flight and are served complimentary drinks and light snacks. A range of business equipment such as faxes, telephones and e-commerce facilities are also available in this lounge.* BA

destinations in 66 countries. In BA name only, it serves 87 destinations from Gatwick in 56 countries, 47 of these being long-haul destinations. BA's partners at Gatwick (including CityFlyer), serve 40 destinations in 15 countries. BA now carries over 9 million passengers a year through the airport compared with 3 million in 1990 and in the same period the number of people it employs there has increased from 2,000 to 10,000.

British Airways, along with American Airlines, Canadian Airlines, Cathay Pacific Airways and Qantas Airways, implemented the **one**world™ global alliance on 1 February 1998. These five airlines between them carry over 174 million passengers annually. Since then, several other airlines have aspired to join this global alliance, including Finnair, LanChile, Iberia and Aer Lingus.

Further information can be obtained from BA's press office web site at: www.britishairways.com/press

CityFlyer Express

CityFlyer Express was formed in 1991 at Gatwick by a nucleus of former staff from the British Caledonian commuter operation, Connectair, and was initially called EuroWorld. Connectair was founded at Gatwick in 1984 and had been taken over by Air Europe and, together with Guernsey Airlines, which had been sold off following its purchase by Aurigny Air Services in the Channel Islands, became Air Europe Express in 1988. It was then integrated into the parent company Air Europe, but this became bankrupt and ceased operations in March 1991. The five senior and founding staff of EuroWorld/CityFlyer were Chief Executive Robert Wright, Managing Director Bradley (Brad) Burgess, Financial Director Chris Simpson, Operations Director Jim Bond and, appointed in June 1992, Commercial Director Malcolm Couper.

The initial aircraft of EuroWorld were two Shorts 360s and the airline's first revenue-earning flight was by G-BNBD, flown from Gatwick to Liverpool on 8 May 1991 carrying mail. Take-off was just a few hours after the airline received its Air

Above: *CityFlyer Express Shorts 360 G-MAXW in March 1992, with Transavia Boeing 737-200 PH-TVH, on a very wet ramp next to the main 'finger' of the South Terminal now more frequently occupied by the wide-bodies of Continental and American Airlines. Geoffrey P. Jones*

Operator's Certificate (AOC) from the Civil Aviation Authority (CAA).

Passenger-carrying flights commenced in August 1991 and at the same time it dropped the EWD flight numbers it had been using and adopted a code-sharing scheme with British Airways for its first three scheduled services, all from Gatwick. These were to Antwerp, Guernsey and Rotterdam, all routes previously flown from Gatwick by Air Europe Express.

Within 12 months of start-up the airline's name was changed to CityFlyer Express, it had the fourth largest number of landing and take-off slots at Gatwick and introduced the first of a new type of commuter aircraft to airline service in the UK. This aircraft was the French/Italian-built ATR-42, CityFlyer initially ordering two aircraft (G-BUEA and 'EB), delivered in the summer of 1992.

CityFlyer was operating the Gatwick-Guernsey route alongside Jersey European (JEA) and was also licensed on the Gatwick-Jersey route, this time alongside Dan-Air. It was also awarded a Gatwick-Leeds/Bradford route licence soon after. These were the roots from which CityFlyer grew, to become Gatwick's second busiest airline in terms of aircraft movements by the late 1990s, behind BA.

In July 1993, CityFlyer pioneered the airline franchise operation, becoming a British Airways Express airline. Its routes had already been established on the BA central reservations system. The transformation now meant that everything gave the outward appearance of being a BA flight — the branding, service standards and worldwide marketing — although the pilots retained their own individual identities and all flight crew kept their contracts with CityFlyer rather than BA. In the first full year as a franchisee, CityFlyer carried about 700,000 passengers and by 1997 the total number of passengers carried was up to 1.2 million, climbing to a figure of 1.5 million by 1998/99.

This expansion also saw the diversification of CityFlyer's fleet and route network. The Shorts 360s were retired and more ATR-42s added. On some of the busier routes greater capacity was required than could be provided by the ATR-42 so ATR-72s were ordered. In 1997, CityFlyer took delivery of its first Avro RJ100 (BAe146 derivative) jet. Routes flown from Gatwick now included Amsterdam, Bremen, Cologne/Bonn, Cork, Dublin, Düsseldorf, Guernsey, Jersey, Luxembourg, Newcastle and Rotterdam. Zurich was added in March 1998 as the

Below: *CityFlyer Express was the UK launch customer for the ATR-42. Passengers are boarding G-BUEA in May 1992 for one of the first flights of the type from Gatwick to Jersey. Geoffrey P. Jones*

RJ100 fleet grew to five aircraft. The percentage of 'feed' traffic into mainline BA that CityFlyer carries has always been considerable and therefore the announcement in November 1998 that BA had made a bid to buy CityFlyer outright did not come as a surprise. Despite a considerable number of objections, including those from Virgin to the monopoly it considered BA would establish at Gatwick in terms of services and slots, agreement for the purchase was given on 28 October 1999 by the Secretary of State for Trade and Industry.

This paved the way for CityFlyer's full assimilation into the BA operation at Gatwick. Meanwhile, CityFlyer had added new destinations — Shannon, Hanover and Nice — to its Gatwick-based operation. As far as CityFlyer's fleet is concerned it will only have three ATR-42s remaining by spring 2000 (G-BUEA, 'EB and G-BVEG which is to be disposed of). Its ATR-72 fleet will be up to seven with the acquisition of G-BYTO from British World, and the RJ100 fleet stands at 11 aircraft.

Because of BA's poor financial results in 1999/2000, the rationalisation of its Euro-Gatwick operation will have a major effect on CityFlyer. Many of BA's sub-500-mile domestic and European routes are likely to be transferred to CityFlyer; BA Boeing 737s could also be transferred, and further RJ100s added to the fleet (see History).

Virgin Atlantic Airways

Richard Branson's airline has been a part of the Gatwick scene since its inception in 1984 and the inaugural Boeing 747 flight from there to Newark (New York) on 22 June. Branson was already well known in the rock and pop music industries, having coined the Virgin name for his record label several years earlier. He was approached by an Anglo-US lawyer, Randolph Fields, with a proposal for an involvement in a new airline to be called British Atlantic. Fields's initial proposal was to operate a Boeing 747 service to New York's JFK airport in an all-business class configuration but his licence application for this proposal to the British Civil Aviation Authority was turned down.

Branson, at first sceptical of the idea, decided the airline industry was consumer-led, just like the music business with which he was now totally conversant. He decided this was an

Above: Four Virgin Atlantic 747 Classics at the South Terminal Satellite in November 1999, including second from the left, G-VIBE acquired in 1999 (ex-ZK-NZZ), in the airline's new 'silver dream machine' livery, which was first applied to Airbus A340 G-VAEL in September 1999. Geoffrey P. Jones

important opportunity for Virgin to diversify, and despite considerable scepticism and resistance from some of his fellow directors, he announced the formation of Virgin Atlantic Airways in March 1984, and that the airline's maiden flight would take place three months later.

A period of frantic planning followed, largely inspired by Branson's infectious enthusiasm, staff were hired, an aircraft found, licences obtained and staff uniforms designed and tailored. On the eve of the inaugural flight an engine failure of the Boeing 747-287B (G-VIRG), appropriately christened *Maiden Voyager* and leased from Boeing, added a considerable edge to the final frantic hours before the launch of the service.

Virgin Atlantic was 'a small newcomer taking on the giant and complacent establishment', according to Branson. The airline's aim was also simple: to provide the highest quality innovative service at excellent value for money for all classes of air traveller. With the bold, ebullient Branson persona at its head, Virgin Atlantic became the new buccaneer airline, taking over where Freddie Laker had left off.

At the time of the inaugural flight to Newark, expansion plans centred around planned services to Perth (Australia), Toronto, Bermuda and Barbados. Early diversification was a feeder service to Gatwick from Maastricht in Holland, with subsequent feeds from Belfast and Prestwick. As a result the second Virgin Atlantic aircraft was a leased British Island Airways BAC One-Eleven Srs 432 (G-AXMU). This was soon substituted by leased V806 Viscounts, G-AOHT, G-AOYP and G-APEY. The Maastricht-Gatwick service ceased in early 1989.

At the end of the first year's trading — only just over half a year for the airline — the Virgin Group reported sales of £94 million. In the first eight months of operations Virgin Atlantic contributed £19.3 million to group turnover and carried 244,697 passengers.

Miami became Virgin Atlantic's next target destination from Gatwick and required the acquisition, again on a lease-purchase agreement from Boeing, of a second Boeing 747. G-VGIN (ex-N355AS and I-DEMU) arrived at Gatwick in 1986 and Virgin Atlantic services on the Gatwick to Miami route were inaugurated on 19 April 1986. G-VGIN also saw the debut of Virgin's famous Scarlet Lady logo on the nose of the aircraft. This is a 5m x 1.6m (17ft x 6ft) multipart decal that proved something of an innovation at the time and was part of Branson's idea to recreate the habit of wartime aircrews for personalising their aircraft.

Traffic doubled to 556,653 passengers following the inauguration of the Miami service, and this also provided considerable feed for Virgin Holidays which specialised in destinations in Florida, Jamaica, Bahamas, Cayman Islands and the Virgin Islands, all serviced by Virgin Atlantic Airways via Miami. Although the start of Virgin is associated with low-cost travel, it quickly established a niche for its upper class business service on its flights from Gatwick to Newark and Miami. This culminated in the 1986 award to Virgin Atlantic of 'Business Airline of the Year'.

Route licences for new destinations were then added: Boston in July 1987 and in March 1988, Los Angeles, JFK (New York) and Tokyo as well as licence-to-fly charters to Orlando in Florida. Two additional 747s were added to the Virgin fleet, G-VRGN and G-VOYG. Increases in frequency to both Tokyo and JFK in 1989 and the start of services to Los Angeles in May 1990 saw two more 747s acquired, G-VMIA and G-TKYO.

Branson had continually campaigned against what he regarded as BA's monopoly position, both on the North Atlantic route and particularly in its operations from London Heathrow. In 1991, Virgin Atlantic broke away from its operation at Gatwick, when it first won the right to fly from Heathrow, inaugurating services from there to JFK, Los Angeles and Tokyo.

Much of Virgin's subsequent expansion has been at Heathrow and has involved acquisition of new aircraft for its growing worldwide destination portfolio; the Boeing 747-400s and Airbus A340s acquired have all been based there and are rarely seen at Gatwick. Operations from both major London airports accounted for Virgin Atlantic carrying 3.2 million passengers in 1998, resulting in a group turnover for the year of £942.3 million. The airline's 747-200s continue to operate Virgin Atlantic's services from Gatwick, with scheduled destinations to Boston, Orlando (two services per day), Newark (New York), St Lucia, Barbados and Antigua.

Virgin set up a franchised partnership with South East European Airways (SEEA) in 1993 to fly scheduled services from Gatwick to Athens (Greece). A Boeing 737-400 was leased from Air UK Leisure for this service which was inaugurated in March 1993. In October, the service was transferred to Heathrow, but subsequently it has returned to Gatwick as a Virgin-franchised operation, now flown by an Airbus A320.

Another Virgin innovation at Gatwick was the launch in May 1999 of Virgin Sun, initially with two Airbus A320s. This airline was offering flights and holidays to 13 Mediterranean destinations from both Gatwick and Manchester. Virgin Sun's distinctive, bright yellow and red livery is a typical Virgin characteristic which helps it stand out from the crowd. 1999 also saw the first of Virgin's B747-200s appear in the airline's new livery. One prospect for 2000 is the start of Virgin's direct scheduled service from Gatwick to Las Vegas.

In the airline vogue for alliances, Virgin has established code-share agreements with Continental Airlines, Malaysia Airlines and British Midland, and has a marketing agreement with Ansett in Australia. Early in 2000 Singapore Airlines acquired a major stake in Virgin. From the modest number of passengers carried by the embryo airline in its first year of operation, Virgin Atlantic has celebrated its 15th anniversary and is now carrying over 3.2 million passengers per annum. Gatwick Airport and Virgin have been inextricably linked throughout the history of the airline and its administrative headquarters are located in Crawley, close to Gatwick. It is also achieving close to 25% or more of the market share on its services from London (both Gatwick and Heathrow) to New York (JFK and Newark), Florida (Orlando and Miami), Los Angeles, Boston, San Francisco, Barbados, St Lucia and Antigua.

Left: *Greek airline, South East European Airlines, leased this Air UK Leisure Boeing 737-400, G-UKLB, in 1993, established a franchise agreement with Virgin and commenced operation of daily Athens to Gatwick schedules.*
Geoffrey P. Jones

Aircraft Maintenance

There are two main organisations at Gatwick which keep the majority of airlines and their aircraft serviced, maintained and operational.

Airliner maintenance can be broken down into a series of checks:

Line Maintenance Check — daily, rectifying operational snags, faults, etc.

A Check — a short, monthly overhaul of certain items following a given number of flying hours.

B Check — now largely dispensed with and combined in a C Check.

C Check — more significant overhaul work that can be broken down into C1, C2 and C3 Checks depending on the maintenance record of the aircraft and what is required and the depth of overhaul.

D Check — deep maintenance with major components being removed from an aircraft for refurbishment or replacement.

British Airways Maintenance

British Airways Engineering airline-wide employs some 9,000 staff at over 100 locations around the world including a large facility on the south side of Gatwick Airport. This occupies part of the former maintenance facilities of British United

Airways, built in the early 1960s and is now one of BA's four main on-airport maintenance bases in the UK. There is an arrangement with FLS Aerospace which leases part of this facility (the former British Caledonian maintenance hangar on the south side) in exchange for BA's use of their large, ex-Dan-Air hangar alongside the control tower (see FLS overleaf).

Nestling amongst BA's premises on the south side is a temporary CityFlyer Express facility. BA Engineering at Gatwick carries out everything from a Transit Check — equivalent to a line-maintenance check — right through to a Major Service Check (after 24,000 flying hours) or D Check. These keep the 70 BA aircraft currently on base at Gatwick safe and reliable.

BA also operates a considerable number of two-man and four-man maintenance teams at Gatwick which carry out diagnostic maintenance on small, unserviceable items during an aircraft turnround. The four-man teams carry out Ramp 1 Checks (Transit Checks) while the aircraft is on the ramp, including a check

Below: *BA's huge, south-side engineering and maintenance base at Gatwick, November 1999. Geoffrey P. Jones*

Above: *British Caledonian's Boeing 747 G-BJXN during a major overhaul in the airline's south-side maintenance facility in November 1985. Geoffrey P. Jones*

on engine oil levels, tyre pressures, aircraft external lighting and cabin emergency equipment, engine health monitoring systems and assessment of the aircraft Captain's technical log entries. These teams also perform the slightly more in-depth Ramp 2 Check, required on each BA aircraft after 190 flying hours. As well as the items from the Ramp 1 Check, they check the aircraft's auxiliary power unit and component and engine component oil levels, cabin interior condition, and the windows.

It is widely believed that in future BA will try to contract-out a larger proportion of its aircraft maintenance and engineering.

FLS Aerospace

FLS Aerospace is a wholly owned subsidiary of FLS Industries and now employs over 3,000 people, 50% of them based in Eire, but the rest at the 11 other airport facilities around the UK and in Scandinavia. Although BA has a larger infrastructure at Gatwick, FLS (the initials come from the Danish founding fathers, Fredrick, Lassoe and Smidth) is none the less of vital importance to many of the airlines using Gatwick. FLS's activities can be split into four groups at present:

• Aircraft overhaul

• Aircraft management

• Component supply management

• Component overhaul and repair

Gatwick's operation by FLS is dedicated to aircraft management generally on the lighter maintenance side, including *live* operational aircraft. This means FLS may have an aircraft in one of its hangars for less than one hour while some snag diagnosis and rectification takes place. The heavy aircraft overhaul work done by FLS is centred on facilities at Stansted, Manchester and Dublin. The Irish operation was acquired from Aer Lingus's TEAM (the experts in aircraft maintenance) in December 1998.

The main role of FLS at Gatwick is a huge line maintenance operation, employing 140 engineers, with mainly small mobile teams running from aircraft to aircraft on stand during their turnround, perhaps changing a light bulb or even a tyre. They also deal with a range of support functions such as de-icing and aircraft handling. Much of FLS's work is carried out at night, with 35 engineers assigned to its night-time contract work on Continental Airlines DC-10s and a further 55 running the line operation. The rest of FLS's Gatwick engineering staff run its day-time teams. FLS now gives line maintenance support to as many as 380 different aircraft for 44 customers group-wide.

FLS's beige-colour hangar on the northern side of the runway, and alongside the new control tower, is one of Gatwick's most prominent buildings. It was built by Dan-Air Engineering in 1990. With the demise of Dan-Air in November 1992 it was closed, mothballed and the labour force made redundant. FLS acquired the facility and reopened it in 1997 following a call from the PR agents for Pepsi-Cola. They wanted a facility at Gatwick in which to house and spray a Concorde in Pepsi colours for a huge advertising promotion. In six weeks, the hangar was cleaned and reactivated by FLS to meet the requirements of the Pepsi contract. Fortuitously, at the same time, BA had aircraft maintenance capacity problems in its south-side hangars and had signed a maintenance contract with Continental Airlines for A Checks on its Douglas DC-10 aircraft at Gatwick. Although FLS has no tie-up with BA, it won a sub-contract for this DC-10 work and swapped facilities with BA. Thus in late 1999 FLS was carrying out Continental DC-10 maintenance on behalf of BA in the south-side hangars while on the north side, BA was using the former Dan-Air hangar, mainly for Boeing 777 maintenance.

Even though Continental is now flying Boeing 777s to Gatwick, one of its DC-10s arrives nightly at 22.00hrs on a flight from Houston. Thirty-five of Continental's fleet of 50 DC-10s are given an A Check by FLS at Gatwick. After arrival, the aircraft is moved to the FLS facility and is ready by 08.00hrs the following morning on standby in case one of its other aircraft goes 'tech'. Its scheduled use is for the 15.00hrs flight to New York (Newark). A different Continental DC-10 rotates through FLS's Gatwick facility on this basis every night.

FLS has signed various deals with many other airlines at Gatwick. Two recent ones have been with AOM (France) for its DC-10s and with Lauda Air for line maintenance on its Bombardier RJ200s. FLS's other main customers at Gatwick are Caledonian (now being incorporated as JMC Airlines, with Flying Colours and Airworld), British Airways and its franchise partners and Airtours International. It is actively looking at further aircraft maintenance opportunities at Gatwick with both BA and Virgin Atlantic and to utilize its expertise in dealing with Airbus A320-family aircraft and DC-10s.

As BA discovered, maintenance hangarage at Gatwick is at a premium and FLS would like to have access to more. BAA development plans for Gatwick on the property side are constrained by environmental considerations. BA is known to have applied for planning permission for more maintenance hangars on the north side of the airport, but these plans were rejected. If BA's trend to out-source more and more maintenance continues then its facilities on Gatwick's south side could become available, but this is purely speculation.

Left: *In FLS Aerospace's maintenance hangar on Gatwick's south side, a Caledonian Airways Airbus A320 (G-BVYB) receives diagnostic maintenance to one of its CFM engines. At Gatwick, FLS specialises in engineering and maintenance work on Airbus and DC-10 aircraft. This aircraft was due to be repainted in JMC Airlines livery. Geoffrey P. Jones*

Above: *The 1997 reopening of the former Dan-Air maintenance hangar at Gatwick, now owned by FLS Aerospace, was precipitated when the Pepsi-Cola Corporation did a multi-million-dollar product launch using a specially painted Air France Concorde (F-BTSD) as the centrepiece. FLS Aerospace*

Above: *Continental's DC-10s are a regular sight at Gatwick. FLS Aerospace has a maintenance sub-contract for overnight A Checks on these aircraft which are always to be seen in the south-side maintenance area. This is N14079, a DC-10-30. Geoffrey P. Jones*

Operations

Handling Companies

Each airline operating from Gatwick must have a designated handling agent. Landside, within the terminal buildings, these appointed handling agents provide check-in, baggage handling and special assistance, including help for disabled passengers and flight information. Some of the check-in facilities are operated jointly or exclusively by the airline in question. The four handling agents currently operating at Gatwick are:

- British Airways — BA
  Tel: 01293 666291

- British Midland Handling Services — BMH Tel: 020 8745 4110

- Gatwick Handling International — GHI
  Tel: (North Terminal) 01293 507147
  (South Terminal) 01293 502337

- Servisair — SVR
  Tel: 01293 505589 (Contact can also be made via the flight/general enquiries number, 01293 535353.)

Which of the above handling agents deals with which airline is listed, using the above two or three-letter designator, against the alphabetical list of airlines earlier in this book.

All the big US airlines at Gatwick provide phased check-in facilities, involving security screening and document checks while a passenger is waiting in the queue for actual check-in, seat allocation and baggage check-in. Pre-flight check-in is also available for passengers with BA (and American Airlines), GB Airways, Deutsche BA, Maersk Air and Royal Nepal Airlines at London Victoria railway station.

One of the four handling agents is also responsible for the aircraft airside as well. These services include provision of all the necessary facilities to an aircraft while it is on the ground at Gatwick, such as tow-trucks, baggage handling, cleaning, some passenger boarding and deplaning, etc. However, the handling agent is not involved in provision of in-flight catering, maintenance (see above) or fuelling of the aircraft. In the case of the latter, most of Gatwick's aircraft parking gates are serviced by hydrant refuelling. Fuel is fed to the gate by underground pipeline, eliminating the dangers and the need for considerable numbers of large fuel bowsers on the airport. Instead, the fuel companies use small truck-mounted fuel pumps which are linked up between the pipeline hydrant and the aircraft.

After check-in, Gatwick operates a Fast Track priority route through to the airside departure lounges at both the South and North Terminals. Similarly, a Fast Track routing is also available for inbound passengers through immigration at both terminals and also for passengers holding non-EC or non-EEA passports. This is primarily intended for the Business Class traveller, and provides dedicated parking areas and valet parking, priority security and passport control channels, dedicated Bureaux de Change counters and Duty Free tills and a dedicated counter at the 'Gatwick Express' railway ticket office. The benefits to the Fast Track passenger are estimated to be a saving of up to 30 minutes on the time taken to walk from the car park to the terminal, through check-in and then to boarding the aircraft at the departure gate. Fast Track valet parking can be contacted at: North Terminal 01293 502355, and South Terminal 01293 502348.

One of the largest and best known of the four handling companies at Gatwick is Servisair plc, which commenced ground handling at the airport in 1988. Servisair started business in 1954 as a subsidiary of British & Commonwealth Shipping and was incorporated as Servisair Ltd in

December 1967. In March 1994 it acquired Ogden Aviation Services Ltd which had been a major rival at several airports, including Gatwick. In October 1994, Servisair was floated on the London Stock Exchange and became a publicly quoted company. Throughout its customer base of 300 airlines at 70 airports in 10 European countries, Servisair plc handled 45 million passengers in 1998 and Servisair Cargo handled 700 tonnes of air freight/cargo. Further information on Servisair can be found on its web site at:
www.servisair.se/index_nonflash.html

Air Traffic Control

This is administered by National Air Traffic Services Ltd (NATS) at Gatwick in a completely separate and independent operation from BAA's ownership of the airport. However, NATS and BAA (Gatwick) plc (on behalf of BAA) work very closely together, and in 1997 enabled the total movements at Gatwick to increase by 8%.

NATS plans, provides and operates safe, efficient and expeditious air traffic services in the UK and Shanwick airspace. It also provides air traffic control at 12 major UK airports, including London Gatwick. NATS employs 5,200 people and

Above: *BA Boeing 777-236ER G-VIIS with 'Chelsea Rose' tail colours, taxies past the SMVCR and fire station after landing and is on its way to a stand at the North Terminal.*
Geoffrey P. Jones

receives no finance from the UK taxpayer. It is funded by the aircraft operators who pay for the air traffic services they use. BAA Gatwick's managing director, Janis Kong, publicly praises the professionalism of the NATS team, both in a wider sphere and at the airport. She said recently, 'At peak times they safely handle an aircraft virtually every minute. This approach over the next 10 years will be vital to Gatwick's planned growth to a successful 40-million-passenger-a-year, single-runway airport.'

NATS has to tender competitively for provision of its services at Gatwick. In 1998, agreement was reached with BAA plc for the provision of air traffic services at Gatwick for the following 10 years, including an interim review after five years. This contract also embraced similar services at five other BAA airports in the UK, including Heathrow and Stansted.

What effect the government's proposed 'sell-off' of NATS to become a public-private partnership company will have on both operations and future investment will be closely watched by airport operators such as BAA and the airlines that use and pay for Air Traffic (NATS) services. The government's proposals call for 51% of the shares in the company to be held by private investors and 49% by the government.

The most obvious landmark of air traffic control at Gatwick is the SMVCR or stalk-mounted visual control room. In more traditional parlance this is the 41m (135ft)-high control tower, opened in 1984. This superseded a more modest, 1950s-style tower to the west of the replacement tower.

NATS is responsible for keeping the aircraft flying in UK controlled airspace and safely separated. There are four control centres throughout the UK (London, Manchester, Scottish and Oceanic). The London Area and Terminal Control Centre (LATCC), located at West Drayton in Middlesex, is responsible for the aircraft arriving and departing from

Gatwick, as well as for the whole of England up to the Scottish borders, Wales, the Isle of Man and surrounding seas out to the airspace of adjacent countries.

UK airspace is also divided into two Flight Information Regions (FIRs), London and Scottish. Within these there is controlled and uncontrolled airspace. Most of the commercial flights arriving at and departing from Gatwick operate within the London FIR and fly in controlled airspace. An inbound flight will often be flying in airways, corridors of airspace from 5,000ft up to 24,500ft. Above this is the Upper Information Region (UIR). Air traffic controllers at West Drayton use radar and radio to ensure that aircraft arriving in UK airspace which are to land at Gatwick are safely separated in the airways over the UK to internationally agreed standards (1,000ft vertically or by three or five miles horizontally). In the London area there are two distinct phases of control. The 'area control room' initially provides a service to an inbound flight (and outbound) outside the London Terminal Control Area (TCA), before staff in the 'terminal control room' take over responsibility for aircraft inside the TCA. When the aircraft descends below 17,500ft (5,300m) it is then controlled towards Gatwick (or Heathrow, Stansted, Luton or London City) from the Terminal Control Operations Room, with controllers using 20in (508mm) square, full-colour monitors to show the position of the aircraft they are handling. There can be in excess of 150 movements per hour at peak times.

Approach radar controllers for Gatwick, originally located in the old control tower, have been moved to the LATCC, together with those from Heathrow and Stansted, in a phased plan to centralise operations for greater efficiency and more effective handling of greater traffic volumes. From here aircraft are sequenced as they descend towards Gatwick to ensure there is no waste of valuable runway capacity and that 'slot-times' are achieved.

The Central Flow Management Unit in Brussels is tasked with minimising delays

Above: *Known officially as the SMVCR — stalk-mounted visual control room — Gatwick's landmark, 45m-high control tower was opened in 1984.*
Geoffrey P. Jones

and speeding traffic flows across Europe. Staff at Brussels are supported by staff in the UK at flow management positions at air traffic control centres, including LATCC. They use a variety of computer terminals, including a traffic load prediction device which shows sector loadings up to four hours in advance. A computer-aided slot allocation system allows staff to monitor sectors which are subject to delay and to check the status of individual flights. A departure slot monitor indicates delays to flights at individual airports and gives an overall picture of the traffic control situation across the UK.

Unfortunately these delays are a fact of life in commercial air transport at the turn of the Millennium. The fact that Gatwick's single-runway operation is dealing with over 50 aircraft movements (a movement is a take-off or landing) per hour at peak times, and over 255,000 movements per annum, means delays are often unavoidable. Inbound aircraft wanting to land when Gatwick is busy are passed from the Area to the TCA operations controller

and sequenced and the aircraft will first be directed to a holding stack. Gatwick's stacks are located to the southeast and southwest of the airport, in huge ellipse-shaped areas of airspace between the airport and the south coast. An aircraft in the holding stack will descend slowly, subject to the controller's instructions, before reaching the lower-level height in the stack, being sequenced and released for its final approach to land at Gatwick.

The Air Controller, positioned in the Gatwick Airport SMVCR, only takes over from the Approach controllers at LATCC during the last 10-minute or so phase of an aircraft's inbound flight to Gatwick, usually 10 to 12 miles from touchdown. NATS and BAA (Gatwick) plc Ltd have also worked together to minimise the environmental impact of the airport's operations. There are specific approach procedures at night to minimise the noise of incoming aircraft. NATS introduced a semi-automatic meteorological observing system at Gatwick in June 1998 and routine meteorological observations can now be carried out by staff without leaving the SMVCR.

The fast-rotating radar scanner that is visible on the very top of Gatwick's SMVCR is the Ground Movement Radar, collecting data for the essential ground radar unit also at the tower. While

Above: *Controllers at work in the SMVCR at Gatwick. Only aircraft on final approach and on the ground are controlled from here. Further afield and prior to landing and after take-off, the control of the aircraft using Gatwick falls to NATS controllers located at the London Area & Terminal Control Centre (LATCC) at West Drayton. Geoffrey P. Jones*

scanning this rotates at 60rpm, for although the view from the control tower is spectacular, controllers cannot see every nook and cranny of the airport, even in good weather. But at night or when visibility deteriorates, it is vital for operational and safety reasons for the controllers to know exactly where an aircraft is located on the manoeuvring area (taxiways and runway) and in relation to the myriad of other aircraft and vehicular ground movements, essential for the efficient running of the airport. This scanner presents high-definition visual data on a screen within the SMVCR to allow an aircraft's safe passage both to and from its parking stand.

For a typical flight departing Gatwick, the NATS computer will already have been fed data generated in the form of a flight plan by the airline's operations department. All European IFR (Instrument Flight Rules) flights must file a flight plan with the Eurocontrol Flight Data Base 'integrated flight plan processing system' at Haren in Belgium. This plan is then transmitted to all the air traffic control centres and agencies whose airspace the aircraft will pass through. From this information the LATCC computer will generate a flight progress strip about 40 minutes before the aircraft's intended departure. This strip will contain vital information about the intended flight, including:

- The aircraft's radio callsign ('Speedbird' in the case of a BA flight) and the aircraft identification (either its civil registration or a flight number, eg BA123).
- Radio navigation equipment on the aircraft.
- A computer identification for the flight.
- The aircraft type.
- The aircraft's true airspeed.
- First reporting point after take off.
- Estimated time from take off to the first reporting point.
- Route information.
- Requested flight level.

The controllers in Gatwick's SMVCR receive the strip and, when appropriate, give the aircraft captain the necessary clearance for the aircraft to pushback via a predetermined VHF radio frequency (see Facts and Figures). The Gatwick Movement Controller will then control the aircraft during its taxy to the runway threshold and then pass to the Air Controller for take-off clearance.

Meanwhile, LATCC will already have information on the aircraft's proposed flight. Once it is airborne from Gatwick, the crew on the flightdeck will change VHF radio frequency and contact the terminal control departure controller who will already have received the flight progress strip. Other details will be displayed on the radar screen and the controller will give the pilot initial climbing clearance, subject to other traffic in the terminal area. The aircraft will then pass between sectors until it is ready to leave the terminal control

airspace. As with an inbound aircraft, which first arrives under the control of the 'area control room', the departing aircraft will be passed to area control at an agreed flight level (FL). A flight level is usually identified in thousands of feet, but without the last two zeros — an aircraft at FL190 is flying at 19,000ft. All levels from 4,000ft and above are identified as FLs and all aircraft flying in controlled airspace above this FL operate to a common altimeter pressure setting of 1,013 millibars.

The departing aircraft, now under the control of the area controller, is given clearance to climb to its cruising level. The next air traffic centre along its intended route will already be aware of the aircraft and its intended routing from the information promulgated immediately prior to its flight by Eurocontrol in Belgium. Area control will then pass the aircraft to the next national or regional control organisation as it is approaching the boundary of LATCC airspace.

Just how fast air traffic is growing and the demands on NATS and LATCC can be gauged by the date when the millionth movement of the year is handled. In 1998

Below: *Only two ex-B.Cal DC-10-30s remained in the fleet of Caledonian Airways in late 1999, G-GOKT and G-LYON which is seen here climbing after take-off from Gatwick's Runway 08. These aircraft have been assimilated into the JMC fleet and repainted accordingly. (see pic page 30)* Geoffrey P. Jones

this was on 28 July, some 14 days earlier than in 1997. To meet this demand NATS has carried out many airspace reorganisations and improvements. In 1998, LATCC's vital statistics included:

- Total (last 12 months) movements — 1,697,428 (+6.8%)

- Monthly total record: July 1998 — 167,259

- Daily total record: 3 July 1998 — 5,852

Swanwick Centre

Recognising this unprecedented growth in air traffic, NATS identified the need for a new air traffic control centre in 1986. A survey amongst staff at LATCC resulted in 62% expressing a willingness to move to the Southampton/Portsmouth area. So, in December 1990, NATS acquired 118 acres of land at Swanwick, near Southampton, to construct a £350 million centre with new plant, electronic systems, air traffic control procedures and necessary support logistics. In June 1997 the government confirmed NATS's future strategy of concentrating on two air traffic control centres for the UK: Swanwick is one and a new Scottish centre at Prestwick is the other. Well publicised delays in the completion and integration of the complicated air traffic systems at Swanwick have inevitably led to delays in the commissioning date. LATCC's area control function will be the first to move to the new Swanwick Centre from West Drayton. It will be followed by the terminal control and military control services at a later date. NATS's prime objective in 2000 is for the successful commissioning of what is now called the New En Route Centre at Swanwick.

Numerous other aviation-related service companies, industries and manufacturers operate in the vicinity of Gatwick. To the south of the airport the Civil Aviation Authority (CAA) operates its Safety Regulation Group from Aviation House, Tel: 01293 567171 and the National Air Traffic Service (NATS) operates its Infrastructure Services Department from the nearby Spectrum House.

Airport Fire Service

A semi-derelict Hawker Siddeley Trident is located in a bunded area within the airport boundary. It is situated to the north of the main taxiway at its western extremity, visible only from the right-hand side of aircraft taxying for take off on Runway 08 or from the left-hand side of aircraft just prior to touchdown on Runway 08. Also visible from the right-hand side of aircraft taking-off from Runway 26.

Right: Former BEA and BA Trident 3B G-AWZX is owned by Gatwick Airport Ltd and used by the fire and rescue crews at the airport for emergency practice drills. Photographed in April 1999. Geoffrey P. Jones

The aircraft was acquired from British Airways when it retired its last Tridents from the passenger fleet and is owned by Gatwick Airport Ltd for use by the airport fire service for fire and crash rescue practice. Still in basic 1980s blue and white British Airways colours but devoid of titles.

Other Aviation Attractions

In and around Gatwick Airport there are quite a number of non-airworthy aircraft that are either preserved or used by departments integral to the airport, eg the fire service. The visitor can see most of these from public roads, public areas or from landing/departing aircraft.

Skyview

Located in Gatwick Village, on the fourth-floor viewing terrace of the main South Terminal, Skyview is a refreshing and popular operation at a major international airport, helping with the Gatwick visitors' 'total aviation experience'. Its most popular facility is the viewing terrace itself which has tremendous views of apron activity in and around the South Terminal and its Satellite. Photographic opportunities from Skyview are best in the morning when the light and sun are better which coincides with the large influx of transatlantic airliners. An entry charge is made, with reductions for children, senior citizens and parties.

Apart from the live action, Skyview operates a multi-media show of a day in the life of Gatwick Airport, the perfect complement to this book. There are also two historic aircraft to view, a complete Handley Page Dart Herald donated by freight airline Channel Express, and the nose of a DH106 Comet 2 in BOAC colours, into which the visitor can look and examine the 1950s-era technology of an airliner cockpit. From the Skyview terrace, visitors can also see a DH106 Comet 4B on the far apron, G-APMB, a former Dan-Air aircraft, now painted all-white and owned by Gatwick Handling International and used for practice and training of staff in the ground-handling of airliners.

Other Skyview attractions are a 'cyber-cafe' and the chance to use the internet, an all-action motion simulator ride that includes a Harrier jump-jet ride, a volcano mine ride and glacier run, one of the best aviation book shops in the southeast of England (currently franchised to W. H. Smith), and a Kenco coffee house/snack bar.

Left: *One of the attractions of Skyview is the chance to inspect this Handley Page HPR7 Dart Herald, G-CEXP, at close quarters.* Geoffrey P. Jones

Opening times are generally 09.00 to 16.00hrs in the winter and 07.00 to 19.00hrs in the summer and admission prices are as follows:

VIEWING TERRACE ONLY

Adults £1-50

Children/Senior Citizens 75p

FULL SKYVIEW

Adults £4-50

Children/Senior Citizens £3-00

Family £10-00
(2 adults/2 children or 1 adult/3 children)

Information correct to January 2000. To check details of Skyview, telephone 01293 502244 or Fax 01293 502246.

Skyview Aircraft

XK655 DH106 Comet C.2R (cockpit only) ex-G-AMXA from the Strathallan Aircraft Collection and now in BOAC colours.

G-CEXP HPR7 Dart Herald 209 c/n 195 ex-I-ZERC/G-BFRJ/4X-AHO — ex-Channel Express

Also visible:
G-APMB DH106 Comet 4B c/n 6422 ex-Channel Airways aircraft acquired by Dan-Air in April 1972, operated last service in December 1978 and sold to Gatwick Handling.

Peter Vallance Aircraft Collection

Located on the northwest corner of Gatwick and off airport property, visible on the left-hand side from aircraft on approach to Runway 08 and on the right-hand side when taking off from Runway 26. Near the village of Charlwood in Lowfield Heath Road, with occasional open days and subject to prior appointment only. Owned by Peter Vallance, during mid-1997 there were plans to move this collection to Shoreham Airport in West Sussex, but these were thwarted and the future of this large collection of former British military aircraft is uncertain. A planning dispute with the local council (Mole Valley District Council) has given Mr Vallance a breathing space and in late 1999 the collection remained largely intact. The following aircraft are present:

G-TURP   Gazelle 1
ex-Redhill, G-BKLS, N17MT, N14MT, N49549. Crashed in Nov 1991. Original pod. First noted here in June 1997.

VZ638   Meteor T.7
G-JETM ex-North Weald, Bournemouth, Southampton, Southend, Kemble, CAW, RAFC, 237OCU, 501, Biggin Hill SF, FCCS, 85, 54, 25, 500.

WF118   Sea Prince T.1
G-DACA, ex-Gloucester-Cheltenham, Kemble, 750, A&AEE, 727, A&AEE, RAE.

WH773   Canberra PR.7
ex-Wyton, 8696M, 13, 58, 80, 31, 82, 540.

WH903   Canberra B.2
ex-Hull, Wolverhampton, Abingdon, Bicester, 8584M, 100, 85, MoA, 85, W Raynham TTF, 228 OCU, 102, 617. Second nose fitted to this aircraft.

Left: *Another attraction at Skyview is the nose of Comet C.2, an ex-RAF aircraft, XK655, at one time G-AMXA, but now finished in the colours of a BOAC aircraft. Visitors can view the Comet's cockpit interior.*
Geoffrey P. Jones

WP308   Sea Prince T.1
G-GACA, ex-Staverton, Kemble, 750.

WR974   Shackleton MR3/3
ex-Cosford 8117M, Kinloss Wing, 203,
42, 203, ASWDU, MinTech, ASWDU, CA.

WR982   Shackleton MR3/3
ex-Cosford 8106M, 201, 206 MoA, 205,
203, 206.

XE489   Sea Hawk FB.5
G-JETH, ex-Bournemouth, Southend,
'XE346', XE489, FRU, 899.

XK885   Pembroke C.1
N46EA, ex-Staverton, St Athan, 8452M,
60, 21, WCS, Seletar SF, B&TFF, 209, 267.

XL164   Victor K.2
ex-Brize Norton 9215M, 55, 57, 55, 57,
MoA, Nose only.

XL472   Gannet AEW.3
ex-Boscombe Down, 849 'B', HQ, 'A' Flts.

XN923   Buccaneer S.1
ex-Boscombe Down, West Freugh.

XP398   Whirlwind HAR.10
ex-Peckham Rye, Shawbury, 8794M, 22,
1563F, 202, 103, 110, 225.

XS587   Sea Vixen FAW.2
G-VIXN, ex-Bournemouth, TT mod, FRL,
RAE, 8828M, FRL, ADS, 899.

XV751   Harrier GR.3
ex-Lee A2672, A2760, 3, 1, 3, 20, 233
OCU.

-    Hunter F.51
(marked E-430) ex-Faygate, Chertsey,
Dunsfold, G-9-448, esk.724, Danish AF.
FAA colours, GA11-style.

J-1605   Venom FB.50
G-BLID, ex-Duxford, Swiss AF.

Annual open days are held. Further information can be obtained by sending an SAE to: Peter Vallance Collection, Lowfield Heath Road, Charlwood, Surrey RH6 0BT. Tel: 01293 862915; Fax: 01293 862533; E-mail: pgvallance@aol.com

Useful Contacts and Other Information

British Airways Flight Enquiries —
   BA's own flights 0990 444000
   BA-handled flights 0990 111666
Bus Services —
   Capital Logistics 020 8897 6131
   Flightlink (National Express)
   0990 757747 or 0990 808080
   Flightlink (from London Victoria)
   020 8668 7261
   Speedlink Airport Services
   0990 747 777 or 0345 581185
   Speedlink (from Heathrow)
   020 8668 7261
Car Rental —
   Avis 01293 529721
   National/Alamo 01293 567790 or
   Central Reservations 0870 600 6666
   Budget 0800 626063
   Europcar 01293 531062
   Hertz 01293 530555

Flight Enquiries —
   flight and general enquiries
   01293 535353
Guest Houses —
   see list or write to: Gatwick Guest
   House Association (The Secretary),
   PO Box 103, Horley, Surrey RH6 9FE.
Hotel Booking —
   British Hotel Booking Centre
   — North Terminal 01293 502437
   — South Terminal 01293 504605
Information Desk —
   general information and tannoy calls
   01293 535353
Left Luggage —
   North Terminal 01293 502013
   South Terminal 01293 502014
Parking —
   Long-stay APOCA Parking Express
   0800 626671

NCP Flightpath 0800 128128
Short-stay TFM Parking Services
01293 502390
Fast-track Valet Parking North Terminal
01293 502355
South Terminal 01293 502348
Out of hours 01293 502124
Police Station —
    situated between the North and South
    Terminals 01293 531122
Rail Services —
    Gatwick Express operates every 15
    minutes and provides a nonstop 30min
    service to and from London Victoria
    station for most of the day and hourly
    at night; tel: 0990 301530 or
    www.gatwickexpress.co.uk
    London Rail Enquiry Office
    (Thameslink Information and Connex-
    South Central) 0345 484950
Skyview —
    viewing balcony, multi-media show,
    Comet, Herald, etc 01293 502244

Where to Stay
Selected Hotels and Guest Houses in the
Vicinity of Gatwick Airport

Le Meridien Hotel, North Terminal,
Gatwick, W. Sussex RH6 0PH
01293 567070

Forte Posthouse Hotel, Povey Cross
Rd, Horley, Surrey RH6 0BA
01293 771621

Renaissance Hotel, Gatwick
01293 820264

The Spread Eagle Hotel, South St,
Midhurst, W. Sussex

The George Hotel, High St, Crawley,
W. Sussex RH10 1BS
01293 524215

Langshot Manor Hotel, Horley, Surrey
RH6 9LN
01293 786680

Bailiffscourt Hotel, Climping, W. Sussex
BN17 5RW
01903 723511

Ockenden Manor Hotel, Ockenden
Lane, Cuckfield, W. Sussex RH17 5LD
01444 416111

Belmont House GH, 46 Massetts Road,
Horley, Surrey RH6 7DS 01293 820500

Gainsborough Lodge GH, Massetts
Road, Horley, Surrey RH6 7DT
01293 783982

The Corner House Hotel, 72 Massetts
Road, Horley, Surrey RH6 7ED
01293 784574

Turret GH, 48 Massetts Road, Horley,
Surrey RH6 7DS
01293 782490

Acorn GH, 125 Balcombe Rd, Horley,
Surrey RH6 9BG
01293 820423

Caprice GH, Bonnets Lane, Ifield,
Crawley W. Sussex RH11 0NY
01293 528620

Rosemead GH, 19 Church Rd, Horley,
Surrey RH6 7EY
01293 784965

Masslink House, 70 Massetts Rd,
Horley, Surrey RH6 7ED
01293 785798

School Cottages GH, Rusper Rd, Ifield
Village, Crawley, W. Sussex RH11 0HL
01293 518813

Victoria Lodge GH, 161 Victoria Rd,
Horley, Surrey RH6 7AS
01293 432040

Amersham GH, Radford Rd, Tinsley
Green, W. Sussex RH10 3NN
01293 883274

Logans GH, 93 Povey Cross Rd,
Horley, Surrey RH6 0AE
01293 783363

Vulcan Lodge GH, 27 Massetts Rd,
Horley, Surrey RH6 7DQ
01293 771522

Yew Tree GH, 31 Massetts Rd, Horley,
Surrey RH6 7DQ
01293 785855

The Coppingham Arms, 263 Balcombe
Rd, Horley, Surrey RH6 9EF
01293 782283

Lar GH, 64 Massetts Rd, Horley, Surrey
RH6 7DS
01293 773564

The Old Rectory GH, 44 Alpha Rd,
West Green, Crawley, W. Sussex
RH11 7AZ
01293 611695

The Lawn GH, 30 Massetts Rd, Horley,
Surrey RH6 7DE
01293 775751

Springwood GH, 58 Massetts Rd,
Horley, Surrey RH6 7DS
01293 775998

Horseshoes GH, Rookery Hill,
Outwood, Surrey RH1 5QZ
01342 842719

Melville Lodge GH, 15 Brighton Rd,
Horley, Surrey RH6 7HH
01293 784951

Berrens GH, 62 Massetts Rd, Horley,
Surrey RH6 7DS
01293 430800

Prinsted GH, Oldfield Rd, Horley,
Surrey RH6 7EP
01293 785233

Staith House GH, 22 Russells Crescent,
Horley, Surrey RH6 7DN
01293 785170

April Cottage GH, 10 Langley Lane,
Ifield Green, Crawley, W. Sussex RH11
0NA 01293 546222

Little Foxes GH, Charlwood Rd, Ifield
Wood, W. Sussex RH11 0JY
01293 529206

Echallon GH, 16 Tushmore Lane,
Northgate, Crawley, W. Sussex RH10
2JJ 01293 535432

High Trees GH, Oldfield Rd, Horley,
Surrey RH6 7EP
01293 776397

Blackberry House GH, 8 Brighton Rd,
Horley, Surrey RH6 7ES
01293 772447

(NB. The inclusion of a hotel or guest
house in this listing does not imply a
guarantee of quality or satisfaction.
Overnight prices, services offered and
facilities may also vary considerably.
However, most are members of the
Gatwick Guest House Association.)

Gatwick Airport Shopping

Within the terminal buildings at Gatwick
Airport, the BAA operates numerous
shopping concessions both landside and
airside. In other words, some are
available to any visitor to the airport
while the airside shops are only available
to those air travellers who are ticketed
and have passed through outbound
security checks.

From July 1999, the old duty free,
which travellers from British airports,
seaports, etc had been accustomed to,
was abolished but only for travellers to
the 15 European Union countries. This
was part of the UK government's decision
to abide by the European Single Market
and its scrapping of tax and duty-free
goods for people within the European
Union. However, BAA and its retail
partners at these shops have absorbed
the VAT on goods. This means that the
prices charged are up to 17.5% cheaper
than in the same shops on the high street.
Because of varying duty allowances in
different countries it is as well to check
allowances at airside shops depending on
which country you are travelling to.
Everybody buying goods in the duty-free
and tax-free airside shops at Gatwick has
to show their boarding card with the
destination on it at the check-out tills —
the cashier will therefore know whether
you are entitled to buy the goods relevant
to the country to which you are travelling.
The shops at Gatwick (correct to January
2000) are:

Above: *Despite the much-publicised abolition of 'duty-frees' in 1999 for travellers to the 15 EU countries, VAT-free goods (and duty-free goods for rest-of-the-world passengers) are still sold at bargain prices by the retail outlets in both of Gatwick's North and South Terminal airside departure lounges. This is the South Terminal. Geoffrey P. Jones*

South Terminal
Landside —
Gatwick Village
Accessorize
Karrimor
Bags etc etc
Knickerbox
Books etc
Manchester United
Boots
Monsoon
Burtons
Nine West
Cadbury's
Past Times
Cap Shaq
Post Office
Clarks/Rohan
Planet Hollywood
Superstore
Coral
Sock Shop
Dorothy Perkins
Sunglass
Hut/Watch Station
Flight Shop
The Body Shop
Gamegrid
The Nature Company

Hargreaves Sports
Thornton's

Airside
Accessorize
Principles
Bally
Red Tag
Beach Party
Rolling Luggage Co
Books etc
Storm
Boots
Sunglass Hut
Chinacraft
Swatch
Chocolate Box
The Body Shop
Dixons
The Clarins Studio
Gamegrid
The Disney Store
Goldsmiths
Tie Rack
Harrods
Warehouse
Next
WH Smith
Nike

Wilsons Leather
Our Price
World Duty Free

North Terminal
Landside —
The Avenue
Accessorize
Serendipity
Austin Reed
Sock Shop
Boots
Storm
Burtons
Sunglass Hut &
   Watch Station
Dorothy Perkins
The Body Shop
Glorious Britain
Tie Rack
Hargreaves Sports
Virgin Music Store
Nine West
Whistlestop
Rolling Luggage Co
WH Smith

Airside
Austin Reed
Serendipity
Bally
Souvenirs & Toys
Boots
Sunglass Hut
Caviar House
Swatch
China & Glass
Take Off
Multitronics
Chocolate Box
The Body Shop
Goldsmiths
The Scotch House
Harrods
Tie Rack & Rolling
Luggage Co
HMV
Watch Station
Marlboro Classics
Waterstones
Next
WH Smith
Past Times
World of Whiskies
Pen Shop
World Duty Free

Above: *The North Terminal is linked to the South Terminal by an inter-terminal transit train, travel on which is free, making the journey in around two minutes.* BA

Above: *Crowded main check-in hall at the South Terminal in 1986.* Geoffrey P. Jones